# A MYTH OF SHAKESPEARE

## by Charles Williams

the apocryphile press
BERKELEY, CA
www.apocryphile.org

apocryphile press
BERKELEY, CA

Apocryphile Press
1700 Shattuck Ave #81
Berkeley, CA 94709
www.apocryphile.org

First published by Oxford University Press, 1928.
First Apocryphile edition, 2010.

For sale in the USA only. Sales prohibited in the UK.
Printed in the United States of America.

ISBN 978-1-933993-82-9

To A. C. W.
*who proposed it*

PHILLIDA
*who copied it*

*and* E. M.
*who presided
at it*

# NOTE

THE following verse was written, at the suggestion and largely on the plan of Mr. A. C. Ward, of the City Literary Institute, for a Shakespeare festival; the first part for the afternoon performance, the second for the evening. Its purpose therefore is only to provide a momently credible framework for representative scenes and speeches from the Plays. It does not pretend to be an episodical play, after Mr. Drinkwater's model, and here and there—especially in the scenes relating to the Court—it allows itself a freedom of anachronism which its title may excuse. It contains no thesis of Shakespeare's life, character, or genius, except that he was a born poet and working dramatist. The scenes included were intended, quite mythically, to represent barely possible incidents in his life, passages read to or by his friends, or performances in his theatre.

It was originally intended that the *Myth* should be produced upon a double stage, the inner being separated from the outer by curtains which could be withdrawn whenever an actual scene from the Plays was given, its movement occupying either the inner or the whole stage as seemed most suitable. Speeches or scenes supposed to be read aloud (as in the second scene of the first part) might either be so read by the speaker or delivered by one or more actors from the inner stage.

It is clear that the *Myth* is capable of a good deal of variation. Complete scenes from the Plays might be inserted between or instead of its own scenes—one from the great tragedies, for example, somewhere in the second part; those included here might be dropped in favour of others at the expense of a little ingenuity in altering the verse or providing additions to the *Myth*. For convenience of reading, the extracts printed have been reduced to their shortest, without any implication that each abridgement is all that it is desirable to give in that particular instance. Each is a matter for the producer to decide with the Plays before him. But the natural interest which the authors (and especially the writer of the verse) feel in their attempt cause them to reserve the dramatic rights; applications for permission to produce the *Myth* as it stands or to make any alterations should be made to the Publisher.

# CONTENTS

PART II

# LIST OF CHARACTERS

*In the* MYTH                    *In the* SCENES *from the* PLAYS

Shakespeare.

PART I.    SCENE I

Quince, Bottom, Snout,
Starveling, Flute, Snug.

SCENE II

Marlowe, Henslowe,          Cosroes, Tamburlaine,
Greene.                     Theridamas, Techelles,
                            Usumcasane; Lorenzo,
                            Jessica, Musicians, Portia,
                            Nerissa.

SCENE III

Marlowe.                    Romeo, Friar Laurence,
                            Balthasar, Juliet, Watch-
                            men, Page; Falstaff, Gads-
                            hill, Bardolph, Poins, Peto.

SCENE IV

Henslowe, A Stage-hand,     Katharina, Grumio, Petru-
Southampton, Raleigh,       chio, Hortensio, Tailor,
Mary Fitton.                Haberdasher.

SCENE V

Actors, Elizabeth, South-     Chorus in *Henry V*, Cleo-
ampton, Raleigh, Burbage,     patra, Charmian, Iras, Dola-
Mary Fitton.                  bella, Guardsmen, Clown.

PART II.    SCENE I

Francis Beaumont, David     Priam, Hector, Troilus,
Nicholas.                   Paris, Helenus, Ulysses,
                            Cressida, Diomedes, Ther-
                            sites.

SCENE II

Ben Jonson, Burbage,     Sir Toby Belch, Sir An-
Singers.                 drew Aguecheek, Clown,
                         Maria.

SCENE III

Burbage, Heneage.     Ariel, Prospero, Miranda,
                      Ferdinand, Iris, Ceres,
                      Juno, Nymphs and Reap-
                      ers, Caliban, Stephano,
                      Trinculo, Spirits.

SCENE IV

                      Autolycus, Clown, Shep-
                      herd, Perdita, Florizel,
                      Dorcas, Mopsa.

EPILOGUE

John Hall, Ben Jonson.

## PROLOGUE

COURTEOUS and kind, hear what we do not do;
We are no learnèd wits, to bring to view
The outward Shakespeare, giving you to scan
London, the boards, the equipage, the man
In every point accoutred to the time;
Nor in the limits of a plausible rhyme
To bid yet more interpretations start
Out of the unknown point that was his heart.
This is but fabulous dreaming; take it so.
We tell you nothing that you do not know.
If you mislike it and are wroth therewith,
O think we call it nothing but a myth.
If here a month and there a name's awry,
O ask but if we do it prettily.
We to the imaging of him to-day
Bring nothing worthy to be called a play;
'Tis but a masque done in his honour—sit,
And if you rise too much displeased with it,
Too much offended by the cloudy sense
Wherewith we sully his magnificence,
Think that by so much you are less than he
Who would have ta'en our service generously.
The younger and the older Shakespeares would
Have willed at least to try to find it good;
Now, though excuse shall bid them be at odds,
Must churchfolk be more godlike than their gods?
Sit then and watch; and if you like our scene,
Say no more than *Thus Shakespeare might have been.*

PART I

## SCENE I

### THE ROAD FROM STRATFORD TO LONDON

[SHAKESPEARE sitting on a stile singing. BOTTOM and the other craftsmen from the *Midsummer Night's Dream* cross the stage, followed after a moment's interval by QUINCE, who pauses on seeing SHAKESPEARE]

QUINCE: God bless you, master. What makes life so gay?

SHAKESPEARE: Rhyme and an empty purse and hark-away!

QUINCE: An empty purse and hark-away? 'Tis so
 That many feel an east wind.

SHAKESPEARE.              If it blow,
 Why should rough melancholy freeze the time?
 Tell me but that—but lest you spoil the rhyme
 I end the line: ah, and begin another.

QUINCE [trying to rhyme]: Well done. When I was young
 and had a mother—
 I made a-many and was spry at fairs—
 But now, God bless us!

SHAKESPEARE:           Now's a pack of cares
 If we will let it be so, but what part
 Can any play to ruin him at heart?

QUINCE: Young blood, young song, young talk, young
 legs on the road!
 But there's a time when all the blood has flowed
 Out of the heart, and though we still write plays,
 As I do, there's a frost upon our days—
 And tragic masks are meant for us to wear
 When—when—when—            [He breaks down

SHAKESPEARE:          O come, devil take despair!
 When we search larders and find nothing there,
 When spry October leaves the hedges bare,
 When we sit down before the fire and stare,

B

When knells of stormy death are in the air,
When darkness swallows all bright things and rare,
When we have lost our hearts and know not where,
When doleful Winter takes the elbow chair,
When thoughts fly up as pheasants at a scare,
When every doublet has a length-long tear,
When—

QUINCE: Ah, you've got a knack at finding rhymes—
That's like me. . . . Did you ever write a play?
SHAKESPEARE: Something of one.
QUINCE:            M'm. Where are you going now?
SHAKESPEARE: London; where else? London, where poets
    are
And plays and theatres and all bright things else—
Except for Anne.
QUINCE:            Ah boy, there's always Anne.
Howe'er we trudge and thrive in London town
There's always Anne in the country pulls us back.
SHAKESPEARE: Well, she'll do better if I thrive. I shall;
And she shall own the biggest house there is
In Stratford, and think scorn of farmers' wives.
QUINCE: That's well; but count your crowns and keep
    them safe.
Don't lend; don't borrow; look askance at drabs.
Don't bluster, but be firm and keep your word.
You'll soon be capped in Stratford . . . Ere you go,
Spend a night here with me and see a play.
SHAKESPEARE: A play! What company? the Lord Cham-
    berlain's? No,
They're to the west. Who acts? and what's the play?
QUINCE: My play; the company's our own. My lad,
You won't find better actors up in town—

Perhaps not better plays. I don't say so,
But others might, and do. What are you called?
SHAKESPEARE: My name is William Shakespeare.
QUINCE:                                    A round name,
A good, no-flourishing, prosperous, solid name.
Come up then, Master Shakespeare; we rehearse
In the forest here,—you'll learn a trick or two
For when you write plays for the Queen's own Grace;
Ha, ha, ha! there, don't mind me. My name's Quince.
This way; this way—La, they're all waiting us.
SHAKESPEARE [while QUINCE speaks to the players]: Fair
    omen! help me, Fortune! These are they
That are half-woodland and half-town; they are
The very stuff of the mind. Up, mind, and watch!
Plays for the Queen's Grace! a true word, my Quince;
But that's to come. Meanwhile, there's nought so
    poor
That has not something in it more than I,
Worth watching, learning, knowing, making fast.
Rare fellows! look, they scatter—Ho, the play!
BOTTOM: *Are we all met?*
QUINCE: *Pat, pat; and here's a marvellous convenient place*
    *for our rehearsal. This green plot shall be our stage, this*
    *hawthorn-brake our tiring-house; and we will do it in action*
    *as we will do it before the duke.*
BOTTOM: *Peter Quince,—*
QUINCE: *What sayst thou, bully Bottom?*
BOTTOM: *There are things in this comedy of Pyramus and*
    *Thisby that will never please. First, Pyramus must draw*
    *a sword to kill himself, which the ladies cannot abide. How*
    *answer you that?*
SNOUT: *By'r lakin, a parlous fear.*

STARVELING: *I believe we must leave the killing out, when all is done.*

BOTTOM: *Not a whit: I have a device to make all well. Write me a prologue; and let the prologue seem to say, we will do no harm with our swords, and that Pyramus is not killed indeed; and, for the more better assurance, tell them that I, Pyramus, am not Pyramus, but Bottom the weaver: this will put them out of fear.*

QUINCE: *Well, we will have such a prologue, and it shall be written in eight and six.*

BOTTOM: *No, make it two more: let it be written in eight and eight.*

SNOUT: *Will not the ladies be afeard of the lion?*

STARVELING: *I fear it, I promise you.*

BOTTOM: *Masters, you ought to consider with yourselves: to bring in,—God shield us!—a lion among ladies, is a most dreadful thing; for there is not a more fearful wild-fowl than your lion living, and we ought to look to it.*

SNOUT: *Therefore, another prologue must tell he is not a lion.*

BOTTOM: *Nay, you must name his name, and half his face must be seen through the lion's neck; and he himself must speak through, saying thus, or to the same defect, ' Ladies,' or, ' Fair ladies,' ' I would wish you,' or, ' I would request you,' or, ' I would entreat you, not to fear, not to tremble: my life for yours. If you think I come hither as a lion, it were pity of my life: no, I am no such thing: I am a man as other men are '; and there indeed let him name his name, and tell them plainly he is Snug the joiner.*

QUINCE: *If that may be, then all is well. Come, sit down, every mother's son, and rehearse your parts. Pyramus, you begin: when you have spoken your speech, enter into that brake; and so every one according to his cue.*

PYRAMUS: *O grim-look'd night! O night with hue so black!*
    *O night, which ever art when day is not!*
*O night! O night! alack! alack, alack!*
*I fear my Thisby's promise is forgot.*
*And thou, O wall! O sweet, O lovely wall!*
    *That stand'st between her father's ground and mine;*
*Thou wall, O wall! O sweet, and lovely wall!*
    *Show me thy chink to blink through with mine eyne.*
                       [WALL holds up his fingers
*Thanks, courteous wall: Jove shield thee well for this!*
    *But what see I? No Thisby do I see.*
*O wicked wall! through whom I see no bliss;*
    *Curs'd be thy stones for thus deceiving me!*


[Enter THISBE]

THISBE: *O wall! full often hast thou heard my moans,*
    *For parting my fair Pyramus and me:*
*My cherry lips have often kiss'd thy stones,*
    *Thy stones with lime and hair knit up in thee.*
PYRAMUS: *I see a voice: now will I to the chink,*
    *To spy an I can hear my Thisby's face.*
*Thisby!*
THISBE: *My love! thou art my love, I think.*
PYRAMUS: *Think what thou wilt, I am thy lover's grace;*
    *And, like Limander, am I trusty still.*
THISBE: *And I like Helen, till the Fates me kill.*
PYRAMUS: *Not Shafalus to Procrus was so true.*
THISBE: *As Shafalus to Procrus, I to you.*
PYRAMUS: *O! kiss me through the hole of this vile wall.*
THISBE: *I kiss the wall's hole, not your lips at all.*

PYRAMUS: *Wilt thou at Ninny's tomb meet me straight-way?*

THISBE: *'Tide life, 'tide death, I come without delay.*

[Exeunt PYRAMUS and THISBE

WALL: *Thus have I, Wall, my part discharged so;*
*And, being done, thus Wall away doth go.*          [Exit


[Re-enter THISBE, MOONSHINE, and LION]

THISBE: *This is old Ninny's tomb. Where is my love?*

LION [roaring]: *Oh—.*          [THISBE runs off
[The LION tears THISBE's mantle, and exit

SHAKESPEARE: *Well moused, Lion.*


[Re-enter PYRAMUS]

PYRAMUS: *Sweet moon, I thank thee for thy sunny beams;*
*I thank thee, moon, for shining now so bright,*
*For, by thy gracious, golden, glittering streams,*
*I trust to taste of truest Thisby's sight.*
                    *But stay, O spite!*
                    *But mark, poor knight,*
          *What dreadful dole is here!*
                    *Eyes, do you see?*
                    *How can it be?*
          *O dainty duck! O dear!*
                    *Thy mantle good,*
                    *What! stain'd with blood!*
          *Approach, ye Furies fell!*
                    *O Fates, come, come,*
                    *Cut thread and thrum;*
          *Quail, crush, conclude, and quell!*

SHAKESPEARE: *Beshrew my heart, but I pity the man.*

PYRAMUS: *O! wherefore, Nature, didst thou lions frame?*
 *Since lion vile hath here deflower'd my dear?*
 *Which is—no, no—which was the fairest dame*
  *That liv'd, that lov'd, that lik'd, that look'd with cheer.*
    *Come tears, confound;*
    *Out, sword, and wound*
   *The pap of Pyramus:*
    *Ay, that left pap,*
    *Where heart doth hop:*
  *Thus die I, thus, thus, thus.*   [Stabs himself
    *Now am I dead,*
    *Now am I fled;*
   *My soul is in the sky:*
    *Tongue, lose thy light!*
    *Moon, take thy flight!*  [Exit MOONSHINE
  *Now die, die, die, die, die.*    [Dies

     [Re-enter THISBE]

THISBE:   *Asleep, my love?*
    *What, dead, my dove?*
  *O Pyramus, arise!*
    *Speak, speak! Quite dumb?*
    *Dead, dead! A tomb*
  *Must cover thy sweet eyes.*
    *These lily lips,*
    *This cherry nose,*
    *These yellow cowslip cheeks,*
    *Are gone, are gone:*
    *Lovers, make moan!*
    *His eyes were green as leeks.*
    *O, Sisters Three,*
    *Come, come to me,*

*With hands as pale as milk;*
*Lay them in gore,*
*Since you have shore*
*With shears his thread of silk.*
*Tongue, not a word:*
*Come, trusty sword:*
*Come, blade, my breast imbrue:*      [Stabs herself
*And farewell, friends;*
*Thus Thisby ends:*
*Adieu, adieu, adieu.*      [Dies

QUINCE: Well done, my masters. [To SHAKESPEARE:] Now, what make you on't?

SHAKESPEARE: Thanks to you, Master Quince; and thanks to all
You gentle company, who make my heart
Shake with dear pity and enforcèd grief
And mortal terror, such as when the tale
Of Ilium ruining in night and fire
Stirred Dido from her contemplation
Of the sea-borne Aeneas. O you are
The mimics of old Death and outworn Time
And stories of young lovers doomed to die,
Tales that set Cupid weeping; you have stirred
My mother in me, and I cannot speak
To thank you worthily, good fellows all,
Lest tears should choke my speech with misery,
And make you weep as you made me. All thanks—
I can no more; speak for me, Master Quince.

QUINCE: Nay now, no marvel. I was moved myself;
In truth, it is a very piteous tale;
You take it rightly; it is tragical mirth.

BOTTOM: Aye; there's a few things need reforming though;

You keep your hands too still, some of you lads—
Put your hearts to it, thus. You're yet too slow—
QUINCE: Aye, well, we'll do it over times enough
Before we take the torchlight. The night grows.
Come, Master Shakespeare, we're for home and bed.
You'll be afoot with the sun, I make no doubt.
SNOUT: Why, where are you going, to be up so soon?
SHAKESPEARE: London, good friend.
SNOUT AND THE REST:        London—nay, there—afoot
With the sun to London—why there?—aye, why there?
SHAKESPEARE: Because I leave the winter for the spring.
THE OTHERS: Spring, spring in London?—Hey now,
    there's a fool!—
Seeks spring in London—hoo, hoo! a fine spring!
QUINCE: Peace, there; he speaks well.
BOTTOM.                            Aye, aye, very well.
Why, there's the Queen; consider, fellows all,
There's the Queen's Grace. Isn't the Queen the spring?
SHAKESPEARE: O yes, the Queen is there—and all the
    Queens.
The woodland's own Titania must be there;
She never found a voice else, no, nor she
Venus with all her doves. They murmur there,
There are the voices; there is loveliness.
BOTTOM: Well, well, God bless you; I had thought of it,
But none could spare me hence when I was young.
        [The actors move off, QUINCE going with them.
            SHAKESPEARE lingers]
SHAKESPEARE: O yes, the spring; but other lady-smocks
Than grow on hedges, other daisies pied—
Pied, pied, that's it.
    [He drags a paper from his pocket, and writes in a word]

Strange how a word so long
Hides in the arras, till a windy thought
Blows shelter off and scares it into sight.
Pied, pied, of course.

[He mutters and a voice sings]

### I

*When daisies pied and violets blue*
  *And lady-smocks all silver-white*
*And cuckoo-buds of yellow hue*
  *Do paint the meadows with delight,*
*The cuckoo then, on every tree,*
*Mocks married men; for thus sings he,*
                                        *Cuckoo;*
*Cuckoo, cuckoo: O, word of fear,*
*Unpleasing to a married ear!*

### II

*When shepherds pipe on oaten straws,*
  *And merry larks are ploughmen's clocks,*
*When turtles tread, and rooks, and daws,*
  *And maidens bleach their summer smocks,*
*The cuckoo then, on every tree,*
*Mocks married men; for thus sings he,*
                                        *Cuckoo;*
*Cuckoo, cuckoo: O, word of fear,*
*Unpleasing to a married ear!*

### III

*When icicles hang by the wall,*
  *And Dick the shepherd blows his nail,*
*And Tom bears logs into the hall,*
  *And milk comes frozen home in pail,*

*When blood is nipp'd, and ways be foul,*
*Then nightly sings the staring owl,*
                    *Tu-who;*
*Tu-whit, tu-who—a merry note,*
*While greasy Joan doth keel the pot.*

### IV

*When all aloud the wind doth blow,*
    *And coughing drowns the parson's saw,*
*And birds sit brooding in the snow,*
    *And Marian's nose looks red and raw,*
*When roasted crabs hiss in the bowl,*
*Then nightly sings the staring owl,*
                    *Tu-who;*
*Tu-whit, tu-who—a merry note,*
*While greasy Joan doth keel the pot.*

## SCENE II

### LONDON: OUTSIDE THE THEATRE

[SHAKESPEARE lounging and watching the actors enter]

SHAKESPEARE: So, pass, and pass. That's Greene—he's
  got no face
To bring a country-lad to; country-lad?
Boor, rustic. Why did I leave Stratford? Zounds,
Because I saw no way of getting rich?
Because I thought my poetry no worse
Than other men's? Is it or is it not?
It rings as hollow. Fool, to think to vie
With Greene and Nash and Lyly—there's a mind
Apollo's bow might loose at and not miss!
But all this loaded pouch of verse—Chut, lad,
That's temper, merely temper. None the less,
Anne, if you saw your singing husband now
You'd think your chance of New Place something lean.
The tavern's my best hope; there's no chance here,
But a word above a tankard—umph; my purse
Warns me there won't be many tankards more.

MARLOWE [without]: Hola, my ancient! hola, child of Jove!
Hovering about the threshold of this house
As his strong eagle on the golden bounds
Of skyed Olympus! Ho there, take my horse.

SHAKESPEARE: I am no fee'd post, sir. Must Ganymede
Do other service than the cup he bears?

MARLOWE: So, so. [To an unseen other:] Here, fellow. [He
  comes in.] What, my Ganymede,
You think it scorn to hold your master's horse?

SHAKESPEARE: O no! but if the thunder-plated Jove
Disguise his godship in a russet cloak,
Close his vast lightnings in a leather sheath

And walk familiarly with tavern-boys,
Must not his minions wait upon his will
And, though they know him, shrug a stranger by?
MARLOWE: That's the high talk; that's the true theatre
   talk.
Why, God-a-mercy, now our horse-boys brag
As if the Soldan's self of Babylon
Outbraved his viceroys and created kings.
My furbisher of phrases, what best chance
Taught your large mouth the syllables of gods?
SHAKESPEARE: The gods that voice them in the ground-
   lings' ears,
And know their kindred by the meet reply.
MARLOWE: God then or groundling? stand, unfold your-
   self.
SHAKESPEARE: Why, to say god were something over-
   sworn,
And to say groundling something undervowed;
Is there no wingèd flight 'twixt heaven and earth
That might have leave to sing what song it can,
And chance the ear it pleased?
MARLOWE:              Please mine then now
With something subtler than a mimic roar.
I do the roar as well as any lion
Let loose within the precincts, but I know
Excess can lift its head to bay the moon
While she rides spotless.  Come, I go—one phrase.
SHAKESPEARE: Are you a poet and would challenge
   thought
To dive below the seas of memory
And bring a pearl to change in merchandise?
I have forgotten all I ever made.

MARLOWE: I half believe you for that very thing.
 You make them then? You have gone out by night
 To watch where Cynthia with a score of maids
 Makes the whole world fantastic with her song?
 Nay now, stout fellow! nay now, turn not hence.
 Your pardon. I have wronged you.
SHAKESPEARE:                          Never wrong.
 But if you challenge all that claim the house
 To show their title-deeds, your years will be
 As a poor lawyer's, snuffling heavy doubts
 Before the clients shouting at the door.
MARLOWE: Why, truth, I'm not loved overwell within,
 But we must talk. Are you in waiting here
 For anyone but Time that kills the gods?
SHAKESPEARE: On Time that makes his common speed;
   on Luck
 That seems to have slept and left the race to Time.
 I could have held your horse as well as not,
 For all my haste; and better, for my pouch.
MARLOWE: Come in then: they rehearse a thing of mine—
 Pardon the brag. First labour and then drink.
 Come in and listen to me. Then my turn;
 No slipping, we must talk. Pray you, come in.
[They go into the theatre, where *Tamburlaine* is being rehearsed]
COSROES: *Barbarous and bloody Tamburlaine,*
 *Thus to deprive me of my crown and life.*
 *Treacherous and false Theridamas,*
 *Even at the morning of my happy state,*
 *Scarce being seated in my royal throne,*
 *To work my downfall and untimely end.*
 *An uncouth pain torments my grievèd soul,*
 *And death arrests the organ of my voice.*

*Who entering at the breach thy sword hath made,*
*Sacks every vein and artier of my heart,*
*Bloody and insatiate Tamburlaine.*
TAMBURLAINE: *The thirst of reign and sweetness of a crown,*
  *That caused the eldest son of heavenly Ops*
  *To thrust his doting father from his chair*
  *And place himself in the Imperial heaven,*
  *Moved me to manage arms against thy state.*
  *What better president than mighty Jove?*
  *Nature that framed us of four elements,*
  *Warring within our breasts for regimen,*
  *Doth teach us all to have aspiring minds:*
  *Our souls, whose faculties can comprehend*
  *The wondrous architecture of the world:*
  *And measure every wandering planet's course,*
  *Still climbing after knowledge infinite,*
  *And always moving as the restless spheres,*
  *Will us to wear ourselves and never rest,*
  *Until we reach the ripest fruit of all,*
  *The perfect bliss and sole felicity,*
  *The sweet fruition of an earthly crown.*
THERIDAMAS: *And that made me to join with Tamburlaine,*
  *For he is gross and like the massy earth,*
  *That moves not upwards, nor by princely deeds*
  *Doth mean to soar above the highest sort.*
TECHELLES: *And that made us the friends of Tamburlaine,*
  *To lift our swords against the Persian King.*
USUMCASANE: *For as when Jove did thrust old Saturn down,*
  *Neptune and Dis gained each of them a crown:*
  *So do we hope to reign in Asia,*
  *If Tamburlaine be placed in Persia.*
COSROES: *The strangest men that ever nature made,*

*I know not how to take their tyrannies.*
*My bloodless body waxeth chill and cold,*
*And with my blood my life slides through my wound.*
*My soul begins to take her flight to hell,*
*And summons all my senses to depart:*
*The heat and moisture which did feed each other,*
*For want of nourishment to feed them both,*
*Is dry and cold, and now doth ghastly death*
*With greedy talons gripe my bleeding heart,*
*And like a harpy tires on my life.*
*Theridamas and Tamburlaine, I die,*
*And fearful vengeance light upon you both.*
    [TAMBURLAINE takes the Crown and puts it on]
TAMBURLAINE: *Not all the curses which the furies breathe*
*Shall make me leave so rich a prize as this:*
*Theridamas, Techelles, and the rest,*
*Who think you now is king of Persia?*
ALL: *Tamburlaine, Tamburlaine.*
TAMBURLAINE: *Though Mars himself the angry God of arms*
*And all the earthly potentates conspire*
*To dispossess me of this diadem*
*Yet will I wear it in despite of them,*
*As great commander of this Eastern world,*
*If you but say that Tamburlaine shall reign.*
ALL: *Long live Tamburlaine, and reign in Asia.*
TAMBURLAINE: *So, now it is more surer on my head,*
*Than if the Gods had held a Parliament:*
*And all pronounced me king of Persia.*
    [Exeunt. MARLOWE comes forward with SHAKESPEARE,
                HENSLOWE, and GREENE]
MARLOWE: Well?
SHAKESPEARE:    No.

MARLOWE:                    Ah tell me.
SHAKESPEARE:                        Tell you? You must know.
MARLOWE: Did ever poet less love praise for that?
  Tell me.
SHAKESPEARE: I cannot.  There were a score of lines—
  I have forgotten—they went past my ear
  Like bright Apollo mounting on his car
  To his best heaven of radiance; what I heard
  Was no more mortal.  O you have put off
  The last poor soiled flesh of humanity
  And are at once immortal.  Was it you
  That bade me hold your horse? your horse, your cloak,
  Your—anything, to have a hold on you
  And think that you once knew me.  Must I kneel,
  Must I confess you are omniloquent
  And leave the world with nothing more to say,
  No, and no way to say it?
MARLOWE:                    It is good?
            [SHAKESPEARE makes a gesture of helplessness]
HENSLOWE: O yes, it's good; but, Kit, you overshout.
  You're always shouting.  Where's the fun in this?
SHAKESPEARE: Fun?
HENSLOWE:              Fun.  There should be fun in every
      piece,
  Or we lose customers.  Still—yes, it's good.
GREENE: You've got a way, Kit, of beginning scenes.
  I've always said it.
MARLOWE:              Luck, pure luck.
GREENE:                            That too,
  But there it is.  I wish I had the knack.
MARLOWE: O any one can do it.  Why now, you,
                              [To SHAKESPEARE

I'll wager you have half a hundred scenes
Beginning with the big line.
SHAKESPEARE:                    Not such lines.
' Our souls whose faculties can comprehend '
O!
MARLOWE: Brother! But your scene. . . . Come now,
The mere beginning!
HENSLOWE:                    Aye, come now, let's hear.
SHAKESPEARE: Well, I have thought—a maid on the last
    day
Of her virginity—a maid in love—
No—for you are the master of us all.
MARLOWE: Not so far master as to think the noise
Sounds in the farthest caverns of man's heart,
Or pierces the dim silence; there are ghosts
Rise not at such a calling.  Come, your scene.
SHAKESPEARE: Why then—you pardon me?—something
    like this:
  *Gallop apace, you fiery-footed steeds,*
  *Towards Phœbus' lodging; such a waggoner*
  *As Phæthon would whip you to the west,*
  *And bring in cloudy night immediately.*
  *Spread thy close curtain, love-performing night!*
  *That runaway's eyes may wink, and Romeo*
  *Leap to these arms, untalk'd of and unseen!*
  *Lovers can see to do their amorous rites*
  *By their own beauties; or, if love be blind,*
  *It best agrees with night.  Come, civil night,*
  *Thou sober-suited matron, all in black,*
  *And learn me how to lose a winning match,*
  *Play'd for a pair of stainless maidenhoods:*
  *Hood my unmann'd blood, bating in my cheeks,*

*With thy black mantle; till strange love, grown bold.*
*Think true love acted simple modesty.*
*Come, night! come, Romeo! come, thou day in night!*
*For thou wilt lie upon the wings of night,*
*Whiter than new snow on a raven's back.*
*Come, gentle night; come, loving, black-brow'd night,*
*Give me my Romeo: and, when he shall die,*
*Take him and cut him out in little stars,*
*And he will make the face of heaven so fine*
*That all the world will be in love with night,*
*And pay no worship to the garish sun.*
*O! I have bought the mansion of a love,*
*But not possess'd it, and, though I am sold,*
*Not yet enjoy'd. So tedious is this day*
*As is the night before some festival*
*To an impatient child that hath new robes*
*And may not wear them.*

MARLOWE: More, more.

SHAKESPEARE:                    Alas, there is none. Still it hangs
With endings and beginnings.

GREENE:                              'Tis Kit's style,
His very tones. You've heard his stuff before?

MARLOWE: O no, not mine, not mine, but the great
     voice
Of the air, and the age, and us that are the age,
Because we come not singly but are sent
In flights and companies, dropping at once
Upon the greening branches of the earth
To make spring happy.

GREENE:                         It is yours, I say.
He has heard some line shouted outside the house
And loved it—so much as to make it his.

SHAKESPEARE [to MARLOWE]: I will not cry your pardon,
   if that be,
  As well it may be.
MARLOWE:             Pardon! you from me?
  More, more. Not that then—you have others?
SHAKESPEARE:                           Why,
  A scene or so—if you were pleased.
GREENE:                   The time—
MARLOWE: Time! Sir, we speak of poetry—there is
  No other matter conceivable in the world.
  Come, read.
              [Enter LORENZO and JESSICA]
LORENZO: *The moon shines bright: in such a night as this,*
  *When the sweet wind did gently kiss the trees*
  *And they did make no noise, in such a night*
  *Troilus methinks mounted the Troyan walls,*
  *And sigh'd his soul toward the Grecian tents,*
  *Where Cressid lay that night.*
JESSICA:                  *In such a night*
  *Did Thisbe fearfully o'ertrip the dew,*
  *And saw the lion's shadow ere himself,*
  *And ran dismay'd away.*
LORENZO:              *In such a night*
  *Stood Dido with a willow in her hand*
  *Upon the wild sea-banks, and waft her love*
  *To come again to Carthage.*
JESSICA:              *In such a night*
  *Medea gather'd the enchanted herbs*
  *That did renew old Æson.*
LORENZO:            *In such a night*
  *Did Jessica steal from the wealthy Jew*
  *And with an unthrift love did run from Venice,*

*As far as Belmont.*

JESSICA:                *In such a night*
*Did young Lorenzo swear he lov'd her well,*
*Stealing her soul with many vows of faith,*
*And ne'er a true one.*

LORENZO:                *In such a night*
*Did pretty Jessica, like a little shrew,*
*Slander her love, and he forgave it her. . . .*
*How sweet the moonlight sleeps upon this bank!*
*Here will we sit, and let the sounds of music*
*Creep in our ears: soft stillness and the night*
*Become the touches of sweet harmony.*
*Sit, Jessica: look, how the floor of heaven*
*Is thick inlaid with patines of bright gold:*
*There's not the smallest orb which thou behold'st*
*But in his motion like an angel sings,*
*Still quiring to the young-eyed cherubins;*
*Such harmony is in immortal souls;*
*But, whilst this muddy vesture of decay*
*Doth grossly close it in, we cannot hear it.*
                    [Enter Musicians]
*Come, ho! and wake Diana with a hymn:*
*With sweetest touches pierce your mistress' ear,*
*And draw her home with music.*                    [Music

JESSICA: *I am never merry when I hear sweet music.*

LORENZO: *The reason is, your spirits are attentive:*
*For do but note a wild and wanton herd,*
*Or race of youthful and unhandled colts,*
*Fetching mad bounds, bellowing and neighing loud,*
*Which is the hot condition of their blood;*
*If they but hear perchance a trumpet sound,*
*Or any air of music touch their ears,*

*You shall perceive them make a mutual stand,*
*Their savage eyes turn'd to a modest gaze*
*By the sweet power of music: therefore the poet*
*Did feign that Orpheus drew trees, stones, and floods;*
*Since nought so stockish, hard, and full of rage,*
*But music for the time doth change his nature.*
*The man that hath no music in himself,*
*Nor is not mov'd with concord of sweet sounds,*
*Is fit for treasons, stratagems, and spoils;*
*The motions of his spirit are dull as night,*
*And his affections dark as Erebus:*
*Let no such man be trusted. Mark the music.*

[Enter PORTIA and NERISSA, at a distance]

PORTIA: *That light we see is burning in my hall.*
*How far that little candle throws his beams!*
*So shines a good deed in a naughty world.*
NERISSA: *When the moon shone, we did not see the candle.*
PORTIA: *So doth the greater glory dim the less:*
*A substitute shines brightly as a king*
*Until a king be by, and then his state*
*Empties itself, as doth an inland brook*
*Into the main of waters. Music! hark!*
NERISSA: *It is your music, madam, of the house.*
PORTIA: *Nothing is good, I see, without respect:*
*Methinks it sounds much sweeter than by day.*
NERISSA: *Silence bestows that virtue on it, madam.*
PORTIA: *The crow doth sing as sweetly as the lark*
*When neither is attended, and I think*
*The nightingale, if she should sing by day,*
*When every goose is cackling, would be thought*
*No better a musician than the wren.*
*How many things by season season'd are*

*To their right praise and true perfection!*
*Peace, ho! the moon sleeps with Endymion,*
*And would not be awak'd!*                    [Music ceases
MARLOWE: And that's yours too? There's something in
    the style—
HENSLOWE: Aye, that's more like—
MARLOWE:                    Aye, that's more like the Queen
  Or the King of Spain or the Grand Turk or him
  Who rolled home last from the tavern yesternight
  To the guardroom at the Tower.  Are you mad
  To think a poet growing like a tree
  From one seed, solitary, has no trade
  By the exploring imagination, with
  All minds that grow about him? Out, you fool!
SHAKESPEARE: You like it?
MARLOWE:                    Like it? Sir (I speak in form,
  Because I speak no longer to my friend—
  As friend you must be—but to him who read),
  Young as I am, I have known men begin,
  Being drunk with some short passion, to write well—
  Then, either that some other work came in,
  Promising greater profit than their own,
  Or that a press of business choked their minds,
  Or that their wealth or lordship shamed them dumb,
  Or that some new ironical intent
  Of that necessity which works the world
  Made them a spectacle of mockery,
  But some way they were changed and silent.  Sir,
  This may be—since man cannot outreach Fate,
  No, not for all his archings of desire;
  But if this lasts you, as I think it will,
  O then be happy, as you are fortunate

Above most men in this—never to know
An ill so heavy or a chance so wry
You cannot bring it still to blessedness
By breathing it in music.  What of us?
We are your lackeys, holding on the stage
Your chairs until this moment, all our chairs
Being yours for the mere asking.  Sir, believe
That I am Marlowe and I tell you this.

> [He turns away abruptly and walks across the stage,
> meeting a much impressed HENSLOWE]

HENSLOWE: You think it's all as good as that?

MARLOWE:                                   All? No,
I think some of it's trash.  Go you and tell him so,
But I think you and I will scream in hell
Before we meet a greater poet.  Go,
Tell him that too.          [Shouting back at HENSLOWE]
                 And you won't meet one then.

HENSLOWE: You've got a way of exaggerating, Kit.
It comes from writing verse.  Still, if he's good—

GREENE: He'll be the rage, and the only shake-scene too
In the whole town—young upstart!  Peacock's feathers
Stuck in a crow's back!

MARLOWE [having reached SHAKESPEARE again]:  Well,
    you'll come with me?
We can't talk here.  No, Henslowe, none of your craft
To get the man tied down to you by loans.
Come, Master Shakespeare.  'Master Shakespeare'!
    God,
How does one call you?

SHAKESPEARE:               Some men call me Will.

> [They go out]

## SCENE III

### MARLOWE'S LODGING AT DEPTFORD

[MARLOWE working. SHAKESPEARE calling without]

SHAKESPEARE: Kit! Kit!

MARLOWE: Hallo! Come in!

[As SHAKESPEARE enters]

Well, is it done?

SHAKESPEARE: This morning—past one when I finished it.

MARLOWE: Well, you've been long enough.

SHAKESPEARE: I know, but time
Gets taken up with half a hundred things,
And polishing these old plays they set me to
Is the very devil of hack-work.

MARLOWE: You're too long
Worrying over them; cut here and there,
And thrust a new beginning in at whiles,
That's the way I do it. But you work too much
At making a fair whole of bits of bad.

SHAKESPEARE: Yes, well, I like it—if it's touched at all—
Not to be spurned by me or any else;
Besides, our company's got to be popular,
I want more money.

MARLOWE: Hear the romantic young!
A poet in his springtide think of gold—
What would the world say?

SHAKESPEARE: I want money, Kit;
Yes, and I'm going to have it. This is the way:
To polish plays as well as any man,
And have a tag in verse as well at need,
And a play of one's own to hand if there's a chance.
You'll see me own a bit of the theatre yet.

MARLOWE: If I'm not dead first. That reminds me, Will,
  What's this word?          [He turns the MS. over and points
                    This—'The gaudy'—what comes next?
  I've thought of thousands, but not one is like.
SHAKESPEARE: That? 'Blabbing', man; b-l-a-b-b-,
    blabbing.                              [Declaiming
'The gaudy, blabbing, and remorseful day'—
MARLOWE: 'Blabbing'!—You are an insane creature,
    Will;
  'Blabbing'—God's mercy, how do you bring it off?
  Not but I might have thought of that.
SHAKESPEARE:                          Of course;
  I know you might; that's why I put it in,
  Just to annoy you, Christopher!
MARLOWE:                          It's too mad,
  Too utterly lunatic, and too madly right!
  'Blabbing'—hell take you! Well, let's hear the death
  Of your two lovers. Are you pleased with it?
SHAKESPEARE: Yes and no since I stopped a score of times,
  But in good truth, I think so. It's so hard
  To judge when oneself opposite oneself
  Seesaws upon the line one's just set down.
  Here's for you. Romeo's coming to the tomb
  Where the drugged Juliet dreams her death away.
ROMEO: *How oft when men are at the point of death*
  *Have they been merry! which their keepers call*
  *A lightning before death: O! how may I*
  *Call this a lightning? O my love! my wife!*
  *Death, that hath suck'd the honey of thy breath,*
  *Hath had no power yet upon thy beauty:*
  *Thou art not conquer'd; beauty's ensign yet*
  *Is crimson in thy lips and in thy cheeks,*

*And death's pale flag is not advanced there.*
*Tybalt, liest thou there in thy bloody sheet?*
*O! what more favour can I do to thee,*
*Than with that hand that cut thy youth in twain*
*To sunder his that was thine enemy?*
*Forgive me, cousin! Ah! dear Juliet,*
*Why art thou yet so fair? Shall I believe*
*That unsubstantial Death is amorous,*
*And that the lean abhorred monster keeps*
*Thee here in dark to be his paramour?*
*For fear of that I still will stay with thee,*
*And never from this palace of dim night*
*Depart again: here, here will I remain*
*With worms that are thy chambermaids; O! here*
*Will I set up my everlasting rest,*
*And shake the yoke of inauspicious stars*
*From this world-wearied flesh. Eyes, look your last!*
*Arms, take your last embrace! and, lips, O you*
*The doors of breath, seal with a righteous kiss*
*A dateless bargain to engrossing death!*
*Come, bitter conduct, come, unsavoury guide!*
*Thou desperate pilot, now at once run on*
*The dashing rocks thy sea-sick weary bark!*
*Here's to my love!* [Drinks] *O true apothecary!*
*Thy drugs are quick. Thus with a kiss I die.*          [Dies

[Enter FRIAR LAURENCE, with a lanthorn, crow, and spade, and
                              BALTHASAR]

FRIAR LAURENCE: *Saint Francis be my speed! how oft to-night*
*Have my old feet stumbled at graves! Who's there?*
BALTHASAR: *Here's one, a friend, and one that knows you*
    *well.*

FRIAR LAURENCE: *Bliss be upon you! Tell me, my good friend,*
  *What torch is yond, that vainly lends his light*
  *To grubs and eyeless skulls? as I discern,*
  *It burneth in the Capel's monument.*
BALTHASAR: *It doth so, holy sir; and there's my master,*
  *One that you love.*
FRIAR LAURENCE:     *Who is it?*
BALTHASAR:                 *Romeo.*
FRIAR LAURENCE: *How long hath he been there?*
BALTHASAR:                         *Full half an hour.*
FRIAR LAURENCE: *Go with me to the vault.*
BALTHASAR:                         *I dare not, sir.*
  *My master knows not but I am gone hence;*
  *And fearfully did menace me with death*
  *If I did stay to look on his intents.*
FRIAR LAURENCE: *Stay then, I'll go alone. Fear comes upon*
    *me;*
  *O! much I fear some ill unlucky thing.*
BALTHASAR: *As I did sleep under this yew-tree here,*
  *I dreamt my master and another fought,*
  *And that my master slew him.*
FRIAR LAURENCE:     [Advances] *Romeo!*
  *Alack, alack! what blood is this which stains*
  *The stony entrance of this sepulchre?*
  *What mean these masterless and gory swords*
  *To lie discoloured by this place of peace?* [Enters the tomb
  *Romeo! O, pale! Who else? what! Paris too?*
  *And steep'd in blood? Ah! what an unkind hour*
  *Is guilty of this lamentable chance.*
  *The lady stirs.*                         [JULIET wakes
JULIET: *O, comfortable friar! where is my lord?*
  *I do remember well where I should be,*

*And there I am. Where is my Romeo?*          [Noise within
FRIAR LAURENCE: *I hear some noise. Lady, come from that*
  *nest*
*Of death, contagion, and unnatural sleep:*
*A greater power than we can contradict*
*Hath thwarted our intents: come, come away.*
*Thy husband in thy bosom there lies dead;*
*And Paris too: come, I'll dispose of thee*
*Among a sisterhood of holy nuns.*
*Stay not to question, for the watch is coming;*
*Come, go, good Juliet.*—[Noise again] *I dare no longer stay.*
JULIET: *Go, get thee hence, for I will not away.*
                              [Exit FRIAR LAURENCE
*What's here? a cup, clos'd in my true love's hand?*
*Poison, I see, hath been his timeless end.*
*O churl! drunk all, and left no friendly drop*
*To help me after! I will kiss thy lips;*
*Haply, some poison yet doth hang on them,*
*To make me die with a restorative.*          [Kisses him
*Thy lips are warm!*
FIRST WATCH [within]: *Lead, boy: which way?*
JULIET: *Yea, noise? then I'll be brief. O happy dagger!*
                              [Snatching ROMEO's dagger
*This is thy sheath;* [stabs herself] *there rest, and let me die.*
                              [Falls on ROMEO's body and dies

          [Enter Watch, with the Page of PARIS]
PAGE: *This is the place; there where the torch doth burn.*
FIRST WATCH: *The ground is bloody; search about the*
  *churchyard.*
*Go, some of you; whoe'er you find, attach.*
                              [Exeunt some of the Watch

*Pitiful sight! here lies the county slain,*
*And Juliet bleeding, warm, and newly dead,*
*Who here hath lain these two days buried.*
*Go, tell the prince, run to the Capulets,*
*Raise up the Montagues, some others search:*
                                    [Exeunt others of the Watch
*We see the ground whereon these woes do lie;*
*But the true ground of all these piteous woes*
*We cannot without circumstance descry.*
SHAKESPEARE [stopping]: The rest is but the circumstance
   wherein
They do descry them.  Well, Kit?
MARLOWE [repeating it]:                  ' Here, O here
Will I set up my everlasting rest
And shake the yoke of inauspicious stars '—
God, that we could!
SHAKESPEARE:              You like it?
MARLOWE:                              That we could!
Will, was it Love or Death or Beauty spoke
That incantation to you? O I think
It is the very voice of poetry
Calling from a rich darkness; it is death,
Where is the full fruition of our will.
And could your lovers be more blessed to live
Than thus to perish on a bed of love?
SHAKESPEARE: I feel half grieved at killing them.
MARLOWE:                              Sweet grief,
Luxuriating in a bath of sound
Made odorous with imagined loveliness.
Will, is it real or is it fantasy?
SHAKESPEARE: Is what real?
MARLOWE:                  All we mean by poetry—

That's the great question; is it a good game
Played with sweet fellows for companions
With the mere game for gaining, and their praise—
Or is it more—a knowledge beyond earth's,
More than the tales of godhead, a divine
Motion of all our hearts towards ecstasy,
And our blood beating with the beating world?
SHAKESPEARE: Who knows? Ah Kit, that's what possesses
    you;
You never wrote a play yet but your mind
Went out beyond it; mine's the steadier sight—
MARLOWE: Yes, you turn back, you do not love the void,
I do not—but it holds me: the abyss,
The whole interminable nothingness
That opens everywhere on t'other side,
And the desire to ride on it like a star;
I know one day it will swallow me.
SHAKESPEARE:                     Pish, lad;
We are the lords of poetry, not its slaves;
And never so drunk with it but that a douche
Of the common world puts all things straight again.
[A noise] Hark, hark, your world!
MARLOWE:            Yours, yours, but never mine.
That's why you play such games with Falstaff here;
Did you go out with him?
SHAKESPEARE [grinning]:   Before him, say,
And came upon him when he had the gold;
Lord, Kit, you should have seen him run.
MARLOWE:                 Not I;
My heart's all in a bitterness with your world.
Have it in, none the less.        [He goes to the door
                Jack Falstaff, ho!

Come in; here's Shakespeare; come in, you mad wags.
And did you stop the carriers yesternight?
What chanced?

[Enter FALSTAFF, GADSHILL, BARDOLPH, POINS, and PETO]

SHAKESPEARE: *Welcome, Jack: where hast thou been?*

FALSTAFF: *A plague of all cowards, I say, and a vengeance
too! marry, and amen! Give me a cup of sack, boy. Ere
I lead this life long, I'll sew nether stocks and mend them
and foot them too. A plague of all cowards! Give me a cup
of sack, rogue. Is there no virtue extant?*        [He drinks

SHAKESPEARE: *Didst thou never see Titan kiss a dish of
butter? pitiful-hearted Titan, that melted at the sweet tale
of the sun's! if thou didst, then behold that compound.*

FALSTAFF: *You rogue, here's lime in this sack too: there is
nothing but roguery to be found in villanous man: yet a
coward is worse than a cup of sack with lime in it. A
villanous coward! Go thy ways, old Jack; die when thou
wilt, if manhood, good manhood, be not forgot upon the
face of the earth, then am I a shotten herring. There live
not three good men unhanged in England; and one of them
is fat and grows old: God help the while! a bad world,
I say. I would I were a weaver; I could sing psalms or any
thing. A plague of all cowards, I say still.*

SHAKESPEARE: *How now, wool-sack! what mutter you?* . . .

FALSTAFF: *Are not you a coward? answer me to that: and
Poins there?*

POINS: *'Zounds, ye fat paunch, an ye call me coward, by the
Lord, I'll stab thee.*

FALSTAFF: *I call thee coward! I'll see thee damned ere I call
thee coward: but I would give a thousand pound I could run
as fast as thou canst. You are straight enough in the*

*shoulders, you care not who sees your back: call you that backing of your friends? A plague upon such backing! give me them that will face me. Give me a cup of sack: I am a rogue, if I drunk to-day.*

SHAKESPEARE: *O villain! thy lips are scarce wiped since thou drunkest last.*

FALSTAFF: *All's one for that.* [He drinks.] *A plague of all cowards, still say I.*

SHAKESPEARE: *What's the matter?*

FALSTAFF: *What's the matter! there be four of us here have ta'en a thousand pound this day morning.*

SHAKESPEARE: *Where is it, Jack? where is it?*

FALSTAFF: *Where is it! taken from us it is: a hundred upon poor four of us.*

SHAKESPEARE: *What, a hundred, man?*

FALSTAFF: *I am a rogue, if I were not at half-sword with a dozen of them two hours together. I have 'scaped by miracle. I am eight times thrust through the doublet, four through the hose; my buckler cut through and through; my sword hacked like a hand-saw—ecce signum! I never dealt better since I was a man: all would not do. A plague of all cowards! Let them speak: if they speak more or less than truth, they are villains and the sons of darkness.*

SHAKESPEARE: *Speak, sirs; how was it?*

GADSHILL: *We four set upon some dozen—*

FALSTAFF: *Sixteen at least.*

GADSHILL: *And bound them.*

PETO: *No, no; they were not bound.*

FALSTAFF: *You rogue, they were bound, every man of them; or I am a Jew else, an Ebrew Jew.*

GADSHILL: *As we were sharing, some six or seven fresh men set upon us—*

FALSTAFF: *And unbound the rest, and then come in the other.*

SHAKESPEARE: *What, fought you with them all?*

FALSTAFF: *All! I know not what you call all; but if I fought not with fifty of them, I am a bunch of radish: if there were not two or three and fifty upon poor old Jack, then am I no two-legged creature.*

SHAKESPEARE: *Pray God you have not murdered some of them.*

FALSTAFF: *Nay, that's past praying for: I have peppered two of them; two I am sure I have paid, two rogues in buckram suits. I tell thee what, Will, if I tell thee a lie, spit in my face, call me horse. Thou knowest my old ward; here I lay, and thus I bore my point. Four rogues in buckram let drive at me—*

SHAKESPEARE: *What, four? thou saidst but two even now.*

FALSTAFF: *Four, Will; I told thee four.*

POINS: *Ay, ay, he said four.*

FALSTAFF: *These four came all a-front, and mainly thrust at me. I made me no more ado but took all their seven points in my target, thus.*

SHAKESPEARE: *Seven? why, there were but four even now.*

FALSTAFF: *In buckram?*

POINS: *Ay, four, in buckram suits.*

FALSTAFF: *Seven, by these hilts, or I am a villain else.*

SHAKESPEARE: *Prithee, let him alone; we shall have more anon.*

FALSTAFF: *Dost thou hear me, Will?*

SHAKESPEARE: *Ay, and mark thee too, Jack.*

FALSTAFF: *Do so, for it is worth the listening to. These nine in buckram that I told thee of—*

SHAKESPEARE: *So, two more already.*

FALSTAFF: *Their points being broken,—*

POINS: *Down fell their hose.*

FALSTAFF: *Began to give me ground: but I followed me close, came in foot and hand; and with a thought seven of the eleven I paid.*

SHAKESPEARE: *O monstrous! eleven buckram men grown out of two!*

FALSTAFF: *But, as the devil would have it, three misbegotten knaves in Kendal green came at my back and let drive at me; for it was so dark, Will, that thou couldst not see thy hand.*

SHAKESPEARE: *These lies are like their father that begets them; gross as a mountain, open, palpable. Why, thou clay-brained guts, thou knotty-pated fool, thou obscene, greasy tallow-catch,—*

FALSTAFF: *What, art thou mad? art thou mad? is not the truth the truth?*

SHAKESPEARE: *Why, how couldst thou know these men in Kendal green, when it was so dark thou couldst not see thy hand? come, tell us your reason: what sayest thou to this?*

POINS: *Come, your reason, Jack, your reason.*

FALSTAFF: *What, upon compulsion? 'Zounds, an I were at the strappado, or all the racks in the world, I would not tell you on compulsion. Give you a reason on compulsion! if reasons were as plentiful as blackberries, I would give no man a reason upon compulsion, I.*

SHAKESPEARE: *I'll be no longer guilty of this sin; this sanguine coward, this bed-presser, this horse-back-breaker, this huge hill of flesh,—*

FALSTAFF: *'Sblood, you starveling, you elf-skin, you dried neat's tongue, you bull's pizzle, you stock-fish! O for breath to utter what is like thee! you tailor's yard, you sheath, you bow-case, you vile standing-tuck,—*

SHAKESPEARE: *Well, breathe awhile, and then to it again:*
*and when thou hast tired thyself in base comparisons, hear*
*me speak but this.*
POINS: *Mark, Jack.*
SHAKESPEARE: *We two saw you four set on four and bound*
*them, and were masters of their wealth. Mark now, how*
*a plain tale shall put you down. Then did we two set on*
*you four; and, with a word, out-faced you from your prize,*
*and, Falstaff, you carried your guts away as nimbly, with*
*as quick dexterity, and roared for mercy and still run and*
*roared, as ever I heard bull-calf. What a slave art thou,*
*to hack thy sword as thou hast done, and then say it was in*
*fight! What trick, what device, what starting-hole, canst*
*thou now find out to hide thee from this open and apparent*
*shame?*
POINS: *Come, let's hear, Jack; what trick hast thou now?*
FALSTAFF: *By the Lord, I knew ye as well as he that made*
*ye. Why, hear you, my masters—*
MARLOWE: Out, out! you tire me. Will, can you suffer
him?
'This sanguine coward, this bed-presser, this'—
Odd's me, I'll hear no more.
SHAKESPEARE [aside]:          Nay, fair play, Kit.
My game, my game. I leave the kings to you,
Leave the fat knights to me. Come, come, Sir John;
Kit's overheated now with too much wine
Or too much poetry. Back to the other room;
There's something yet to hear—the money, Jack,
How the poor merchants got their coin again.   ·
Of honest gratitude, honest reward,
Whereof some half is yours.
[Aside to MARLOWE]          When you would go,

Call me and I'll be with you.  What, my lad,
It's a fair world.
MARLOWE:            And you—it's you that moan
So sweetly that all lovers stop to hear,
Letting their negligent arms slide from their girls
Because no body's softness is so sweet
As that enchanting sorrow! and you go
To change bravados with a tavern sot.
SHAKESPEARE: Live and let live.  Call me when you would
    go.
Come, Jack, fat Jack, mad Jack! come, brave Sir John.
                    [They go out]
MARLOWE: That's if he holds it; if he doesn't lose,
As some would; if he grows to it, and them.
I can be good hail-fellow with them all
And keep my mind to itself, and let it rage
Within the bars of vigilance, but he
Lets his mind out to saunter with them all,
And doffs his hat in church the good old way
On Sundays, and on Mondays scurries round
To help the property man, and afternoons
Sits taking money at the doors.  My God—
' And shake the yoke of inauspicious stars
From this world-wearied flesh.'—

THE THEATRE

[A rehearsal of *The Taming of the Shrew* has been taking place.
SHAKESPEARE, HENSLOWE]

HENSLOWE: What more do you want?
SHAKESPEARE:                                    I want the thing itself—
Not a bad picture of it. They *will* roar—
See, your Petruchio does it all the time:
Stamping his feet in passion: waving arms
In anger. I want quiet and my words.
HENSLOWE: They were word-perfect.
SHAKESPEARE:                              No, they shook the words,
Bullied them, beat them, thrust them into place,
With Ah's and O's and such like roars of rage
One would think they threatened the poor harmless words
With being instantly thrown out of the play
If they should fail to explode about the stage.
That's not the way. Henslowe, I'll do the work,
I've done it, if they'll only follow on
Docilely; let them sit and walk and turn
And leave the playing to the words they say.
HENSLOWE: You talk of words as if they were living things.
SHAKESPEARE: Yes, with a life not ours. O who can tell
With what amazement words can grow aware
Of their own being, and, once come of age,
Take counsel with each other how to live;
Which are of quality and which are sent
To be the page boys, posts, and scavengers,
Within the common utterance of the world.
Some thrive as lords do, living on the farms
And product of a minstrel's revenue;
Some play the herald and the pursuivant

In tables, charters, and decrees of state;
Some like good traders bring their masters gold
To profit from sea-going merchandise;
And some, like beggars, wander up and down
Snuffing the air in penury and disease,
And come in attics to a kind of death,
Being forgotten of our royal tongue.

HENSLOWE: You talk of words as if they were living
   things.

SHAKESPEARE: That's what you said—exactly what you
   said—
A minute ago. Well, as to the acting now.
If you will teach them just to say the words,
The words will do the play. They shall have scenes
For riot, noise, and women's flutterings;
Let them have wit enough to keep it there.
                              [A stage-hand looks in

STAGE-HAND: Master Shakespeare!

SHAKESPEARE:                           Aye?

STAGE-HAND:                  There's a full crowd without
Of lords and ladies come in search of you.

HENSLOWE: That means no more rehearsal. Plague
   upon't!
Now you'll go hours preening yourself in glee
To be amongst the courtiers, dropping bows
And interchanging affabilities,
And devil take the work.

SHAKESPEARE:                   Don't fear for me;
I put my talent out at market so
And get it back with usury. Who caught
The smile of the Queen's Grace for the Company
But I, my Henslowe?

HENSLOWE: Cloak it as you will:
'Tis your delight, and not your profit, doffs
Your hat before gentility. Why, you prink
Like a shy maiden when the lords come in.
STAGE-HAND: They're coming, Master Shakespeare.
SHAKESPEARE: Let them come.
Henslowe, I make my profit from my joy
Like a bee honeying down a walk of flowers,
And bearing such delight back to his hive
As builds his house the nobler. O be sure,
He loses labour who with a gnarled brow
Wrestling a sweaty hour against the world
Seeks then to pick its pocket. You don't love
The pageantry of honour-ranking heads,
The leoparded dais, and the sworded throne,
All ceremony and solemnity,
As I do; you don't please it therefore. Hush!
    [SOUTHAMPTON, RALEIGH, MARY FITTON, and others]
My lord! [bowing] My lord! Sir! Mistress Fitton! Sir!
SOUTHAMPTON: 'Tis he at last!
RALEIGH: Hid like the honey in bees
In the stomach of the theatre!
HENSLOWE [going out]: Bees again!
I know whom they should sting, if bees were I.
SHAKESPEARE: Much welcome to the lordship of the land
From their mere servitor. Gentles, well met.
And what make you in the poor Globe to-day?
SOUTHAMPTON: Why, thus. The Queen's Grace sends by
    me her will
That your fair company should bring a play
To Greenwich in a fortnight's space: all choice
She leaves to you—' knowing,' she bade me say,

' She trusts her good friend Shakespeare to be clear
From calumny and treason, such as hurt
The fair fame of a queen still fancy free,
And lesser poets soil them with at whiles '.
RALEIGH: God save the Queen! the proclamation's done.
SHAKESPEARE: God save the Queen, and give the Queen
her will.
MARY FITTON: Isn't that you, Will Shakespeare, the
Queen's Will?
SHAKESPEARE: Queen's Will because the Queen's will
made me will
No other Will to serve the Queen so well.
SOUTHAMPTON: God save your willship then, worshipful
Will!
MARY FITTON: And keep your will-full self from wilful-
ness.
RALEIGH: Lest willy-nilly you be 'wildered, Will.
SOUTHAMPTON: Truce, truce, he fails! the joke falls down
at last.
Your forfeit, Raleigh; the last flight went wide.
Well, Shakespeare, shall I bless you to the Queen?
SHAKESPEARE: God save the Queen—so bless me to her
Grace—
What will she have? love scene or history,
Fantasy, comedy, or tragic roar?
SOUTHAMPTON: Something of yours and—harkye! in
your ear—                        [He takes him aside
Something to show how fairly England holds
Her ancient bravery and keeps the sword
That the Queen's sires flashed o'er the foreign lands
Loose in the scabbard. She's in a brave mood,
And talks at large of battlements abroad—

Spain, France, I know not. All is naught but mood,
To change before the moon's out. Have two plays,
One all agog with gentlemen at arms,
One laughing and home-nurtured, country wives
Gossiping 'neath their cows. I'll send you word
What humour takes her and what play will fit.

SHAKESPEARE: God save your lordship and my ears from
  cropping.

SOUTHAMPTON: Nay, but she's placable and she likes you,
  Will;
No need to rouse her, though; no dying Richard—
That went a thought too near. Daily she lives
Eyeing each knife that butlers lay on the board;
Always Elizabeth, but sometimes pale—
No dark stairs in the palace, and no yards
Where the night torches flicker shadows down.
[Aloud] What's on to-day?

SHAKESPEARE:                    *The Taming of the Shrew.*

RALEIGH: Yours?

SHAKESPEARE: Say, four fingers, but the other six
  Some poet's long dead.

RALEIGH:                    Would it had been yours!
Likely you never had a shrew to tame?

MARY FITTON: All women married to poets grow to
  shrews.
Don't they, Will Shakespeare? When the cupboard's
  bare,
And children run barefoot for lack of shoes?

SHAKESPEARE: No woman, Madam, ever turned a shrew,
Unless her husband turned cold morsels first
Upon her trencher; that's when shrewhood grows:
But poets—Will you hear a piece of the play?

SOUTHAMPTON: A moment, Will. But poets—what would
    you say?
SHAKESPEARE: Alas, my lord, I would not boast my
    trade;
 I am but parcel poet; most of me
 Drawn out in plans and lists of properties,
 The honest foreman of a working gang
 Of honest actors. But if you should ask
 What thing it is that keeps a woman sweet
 And a man tender, I would make a guess.
MARY FITTON: What is it then? What book has taught
    you that?
SHAKESPEARE: *O where is any author in the world*
    *Teaches such beauty as a woman's eye?*
    *Learning is but an adjunct to ourself*
    *And where we are our learning likewise is:*
    *Then when ourselves we see in ladies' eyes,*
    *Do we not likewise see our learning there?*
    *O, we have made a vow to study, lords,*
    *And in that vow we have forsworn our books.*
    *For when would you, my liege, or you, or you,*
    *In leaden contemplation have found out*
    *Such fiery numbers as the prompting eyes*
    *Of beauty's tutors have enrich'd you with?*
    *Other slow arts entirely keep the brain;*
    *And therefore, finding barren practisers,*
    *Scarce show a harvest of their heavy toil:*
    *But love, first learned in a lady's eyes,*
    *Lives not alone immured in the brain;*
    *But, with the motion of all elements,*
    *Courses as swift as thought in every power,*
    *And gives to every power a double power,*

*Above their functions and their offices.*
*It adds a precious seeing to the eye;*
*A lover's eyes will gaze an eagle blind;*
*A lover's ear will hear the lowest sound,*
*When the suspicious head of theft is stopp'd:*
*Love's feeling is more soft and sensible*
*Than are the tender horns of cockled snails;*
*Love's tongue proves dainty Bacchus gross in taste:*
*For valour, is not Love a Hercules,*
*Still climbing trees in the Hesperides?*
*Subtle as Sphinx; as sweet and musical*
*As bright Apollo's lute, strung with his hair;*
*And when Love speaks, the voice of all the gods*
*Makes heaven drowsy with the harmony.*

SOUTHAMPTON [after a pause]: See, they are drowsy with
    the harmony.
Why, Raleigh! Sleep you, Mistress Fitton? Troth,
I cannot blame you, seeing I myself
Am in enchantment, not a waking world,
And with a heavy heart must stir again
Out of this loving spell to common things.

SHAKESPEARE: Then let us prologue it with louder spells
Calling the mirth and tumult of a jest
To lead you gently into wakefulness.
Ho there! rehearsal!

[As the actors come in, he speaks to HENSLOWE and then goes back
                to MARY FITTON]

MARY FITTON: And do you talk so to your wife? O Will,
Could she let go such music from her ward
To strum in taverns and in theatres?

SHAKESPEARE: Madam, though Love be wiser than the gods,
He is no conjurer turning stones to bread.

MARY FITTON: Are you not grown a wiser than the gods
  To turn our stony hearts to manchet bread?
SHAKESPEARE: No bread that you could eat, because no
    song
  Can teach Love's godhead what Love's godhead is.
  See, if one star should dip from all the stars
  That with a planetary music wheel
  Within the abysm and deep gulf of space,
  Should you . . . should it . . . hear with contented ear
  The jangling discords of a mortal tongue
  Though blest with sweetness more than Virgil's was?
MARY FITTON: With no content, alas! but all myself
  Lost and enveloped in the harmony!
  The play! the play!

[Enter KATHARINA and GRUMIO]

GRUMIO: *No, no, forsooth; I dare not for my life.*
KATHARINA: *The more my wrong, the more his spite appears;*
  *What, did he marry me to famish me?*
  *Beggars, that come unto my father's door,*
  *Upon entreaty have a present alms;*
  *If not, elsewhere they meet with charity:*
  *But I, who never knew how to entreat,*
  *Nor never needed that I should entreat,*
  *Am starved for meat, giddy for lack of sleep,*
  *With oaths kept waking and with brawling fed:*
  *And that which spites me more than all these wants,*
  *He does it under name of perfect love;*
  *As who should say, if I should sleep or eat,*
  *'Twere deadly sickness or else present death.*
  *I prithee go and get me some repast;*
  *I care not what, so it be wholesome food. . . .*

[Enter PETRUCHIO and HORTENSIO with meat]

PETRUCHIO: *How fares my Kate? What, sweeting, all amort?*

HORTENSIO: *Mistress, what cheer?*

KATHARINA: *Faith, as cold as can be.*

PETRUCHIO: *Pluck up thy spirits; look cheerfully upon me.*
*Here, love; thou see'st how diligent I am*
*To dress thy meat myself and bring it thee:*
*I am sure, sweet Kate, this kindness merits thanks.*
*What, not a word? Nay, then thou lovest it not;*
*And all my pains is sorted to no proof.*
*Here, take away this dish.*

KATHARINA: *I pray you, let it stand.*

PETRUCHIO: *The poorest service is repaid with thanks;*
*And so shall mine, before you touch the meat.*

KATHARINA: *I thank you, sir.*

HORTENSIO: *Signior Petruchio, fie! you are to blame.*
*Come, Mistress Kate, I'll bear you company.*

PETRUCHIO: [aside] *Eat it up all, Hortensio, if thou lovest me.*
*Much good do it unto thy gentle heart!*
*Kate, eat apace: and now, my honey love,*
*Will we return unto thy father's house*
*And revel it as bravely as the best,*
*With silken coats and caps and golden rings,*
*With ruffs and cuffs and fardingales and things;*
*With scarfs and fans and double change of bravery,*
*With amber bracelets, beads and all this knavery.*
*What, hast thou dined? The tailor stays thy leisure,*
*To deck thy body with his ruffling treasure.*

[Enter Tailor]

*Come, tailor, let us see these ornaments;*
*Lay forth the gown.*

[Enter Haberdasher]

*What news with you, sir?*

HABERDASHER: *Here is the cap your worship did bespeak.*

PETRUCHIO: *Why, this was moulded on a porringer;*
*A velvet dish: fie, fie! 'tis lewd and filthy:*
*Why, 'tis a cockle or a walnut-shell,*
*A knack, a toy, a trick, a baby's cap:*
*Away with it! come, let me have a bigger.*

KATHARINA: *I'll have no bigger: this doth fit the time,*
*And gentlewomen wear such caps as these.*

PETRUCHIO: *When you are gentle, you shall have one too,*
*And not till then.*

HORTENSIO [aside]: *That will not be in haste.*

KATHARINA: *Why, sir, I trust I may have leave to speak;*
*And speak I will; I am no child, no babe:*
*Your betters have endured me say my mind,*
*And if you cannot, best you stop your ears.*
*My tongue will tell the anger of my heart,*
*Or else my heart concealing it will break,*
*And rather than it shall, I will be free*
*Even to the uttermost, as I please, in words.*

PETRUCHIO: *Why, thou say'st true; it is a paltry cap,*
*A custard-coffin, a bauble, a silken pie:*
*I love thee well, in that thou likest it not.*

KATHARINA: *Love me or love me not, I like the cap;*
*And it I will have, or I will have none.*   [Exit Haberdasher

PETRUCHIO: *Thy gown? why, ay: come, tailor, let us see't.*
*O mercy, God! what masquing stuff is here?*
*What's this? a sleeve? 'tis like a demi-cannon:*
*What, up and down, carved like an apple-tart?*
*Here's snip and nip and cut and slish and slash,*
*Like to a censer in a barber's shop:*

*Why, what, i' devil's name, tailor, call'st thou this?*

HORTENSIO [aside]: *I see she's like to have neither cap nor*
  *gown.*

TAILOR: *You bid me make it orderly and well,*
  *According to the fashion and the time.*

PETRUCHIO: *Marry, and did; but if you be remember'd,*
  *I did not bid you mar it to the time.*
  *Go, hop me over every kennel home,*
  *For you shall hop without my custom, sir:*
  *I'll none of it: hence! make your best of it.*

KATHARINA: *I never saw a better-fashion'd gown,*
  *More quaint, more pleasing, nor more commendable:*
  *Belike you mean to make a puppet of me.*

PETRUCHIO: *Why, true; he means to make a puppet of thee.*

TAILOR: *She says your worship means to make a puppet of her.*

PETRUCHIO: *O monstrous arrogance! Thou liest, thou*
  *thread, thou thimble,*
  *Thou yard, three-quarters, half-yard, quarter, nail!*
  *Thou flea, thou nit, thou winter-cricket thou!*
  *Braved in mine own house with a skein of thread?*
  *Away, thou rag, thou quantity, thou remnant;*
  *Or I shall so be-mete thee with thy yard*
  *As thou shalt think on prating whilst thou livest!*
  *I tell thee, I, that thou hast marr'd her gown.*

TAILOR: *Your worship is deceived; the gown is made*
  *Just as my master had direction:*
  *Grumio gave order how it should be done.*

GRUMIO: *I gave him no order; I gave him the stuff.*

TAILOR: *But how did you desire it should be made?*

GRUMIO: *Marry, sir, with needle and thread.*

TAILOR: *But did you not request to have it cut?*

GRUMIO: *Thou hast faced many things.*

TAILOR: *I have.*

GRUMIO: *Face not me: thou hast braved many men; brave not me; I will neither be faced nor braved. I say unto thee, I bid thy master cut out the gown; but I did not bid him cut it to pieces: ergo, thou liest.*

TAILOR: *Why, here is the note of the fashion to testify.*

PETRUCHIO: *Read it.*

GRUMIO: *The note lies in's throat, if he say I said so.*

TAILOR [reads]: ' *Imprimis, a loose-bodied gown* '—

GRUMIO: *Master, if ever I said loose-bodied gown, sew me in the skirts of it, and beat me to death with a bottom of brown thread: I said a gown.*

PETRUCHIO: *Proceed.*

TAILOR [reads]: ' *With a small compassed cape:* '

GRUMIO: *I confess the cape.*

TAILOR [reads]: ' *With a trunk sleeve:*

GRUMIO: *I confess two sleeves.*

TAILOR [reads]: ' *The sleeves curiously cut.*'

PETRUCHIO: *Ay, there's the villany.*

GRUMIO: *Error i' the bill, sir; error i' the bill. I commanded the sleeves should be cut out and sewed up again; and that I'll prove upon thee, though thy little finger be armed in a thimble.*

TAILOR: *This is true that I say: an I had thee in place where, thou shouldst know it.*

GRUMIO: *I am for thee straight: take thou the bill, give me thy mete-yard, and spare not me.*

HORTENSIO: *God-a-mercy, Grumio! then he shall have no odds.*

PETRUCHIO: *Well, sir, in brief, the gown is not for me.*
[Aside] *Hortensio, say thou wilt see the tailor paid.*
*Go, take it hence; be gone, and say no more.*

HORTENSIO: *Tailor, I'll pay thee for thy gown to-morrow:*

E

*Take no unkindness of his hasty words:*
*Away! I say; commend me to thy master.* [Exit Tailor
PETRUCHIO: *Well, come, my Kate; we will unto your father's*
*Even in these honest mean habiliments:*
*Our purses shall be proud, our garments poor;*
*For 'tis the mind that makes the body rich;*
*And as the sun breaks through the darkest clouds,*
*So honour peereth in the meanest habit.*
*What is the jay more precious than the lark,*
*Because his feathers are more beautiful?*
*Or is the adder better than the eel,*
*Because his painted skin contents the eye?*
*O, no, good Kate; neither art thou the worse*
*For this poor furniture and mean array.*
*If thou account'st it shame, lay it on me;*
*And therefore frolic: we will hence forthwith,*
*To feast and sport us at thy father's house.*
*Go, call my men, and let us straight to him;*
*And bring our horses unto Long-lane end;*
*There will we mount, and thither walk on foot.*
*Let's see; I think 'tis now some seven o'clock,*
*And well we may come there by dinner-time.*
KATHARINA: *I dare assure you, sir, 'tis almost two;*
*And 'twill be supper-time ere you come there.*
PETRUCHIO: *It shall be seven ere I go to horse:*
*Look, what I speak, or do, or think to do,*
*You are still crossing it. Sirs, let't alone:*
*I will not go to-day; and ere I do,*
*It shall be what o'clock I say it is.*
HORTENSIO [aside]: *Why, so this gallant will command*
    *the sun.* [Exeunt
        [The courtiers rise amid a confusion of voices]

SOUTHAMPTON: O the strong fellow!

RALEIGH:                  O the peevish wench!

MARY FITTON [to SHAKESPEARE, as she rises]: What, must
   you sing me into insolence
Because of my own greatness? and then scourge
That insolence from me with o'er-riding oaths?
Must I be yours?

SHAKESPEARE:      Who bids you to be mine?
  Because I cannot look away from you,
  Is that a reason you should look on me?—
  My lord!

SOUTHAMPTON: A gay hour, but your debtors for it
  Must be your debtors, and must mount and ride.

RALEIGH: Leaving our laughter for your only pay.

MARY FITTON [apart to SHAKESPEARE]: Poor payers make
   good givers. I shall dream
To-night that you have stripped my gown away.

SHAKESPEARE [apart to her]: Dream that all lovers know
   a better wear—
Nay, let me serve your lordship. Gentlemen . . .

                                   [They go out

SOUTHAMPTON [without]: No farther, Will: we hinder
   you too long;
Nay, you shall back.

SHAKESPEARE [without]: My dear lord! . . All, farewell!

[SHAKESPEARE, returning alone, walks meditatively up and down
  two or three times; then he takes out several papers and looks
  at them. He sits down and reads aloud:]

*Whoever hath her wish, thou hast thy* Will,
*And* Will *to boot, and* Will *in over-plus;*
*More than enough am I that vex thee still,*
*To thy sweet will making addition thus.*

*Wilt thou, whose will is large and spacious,*
*Not once vouchsafe to hide my will in thine?*
*Shall will in others seem right gracious,*
*And in my will no fair acceptance shine?*
*The sea, all water, yet receives rain still,*
*And in abundance addeth to his store;*
*So thou, being rich in* Will, *add to thy* Will
*One will of mine, to make thy large* Will *more.*
   *Let no unkind ' No ' fair beseechers kill;*
   *Think all but one, and me in that one* Will.

*In the old age black was not counted fair,*
*Or if it were, it bore not beauty's name;*
*But now is black beauty's successive heir,*
*And beauty slander'd with a bastard's shame:*
*For since each hand hath put on Nature's power,*
*Fairing the foul with Art's false borrow'd face,*
*Sweet beauty hath no name, no holy bower,*
*But is profan'd, if not lives in disgrace.*
*Therefore my mistress' brows are raven black,*
*Her eyes so suited, and they mourners seem*
*At such who, not born fair, no beauty lack,*
*Sland'ring creation with a false esteem:*
   *Yet so they mourn, becoming of their woe,*
   *That every tongue says beauty should look so.*

*In faith, I do not love thee with mine eyes,*
*For they in thee a thousand errors note;*
*But 'tis my heart that loves what they despise,*
*Who* (ta ti ta ti ta) *is pleas'd to dote.*
   [As he stops to make an insertion the curtain falls]

## SCENE V

## THE COURT

[An ante-chamber opening on a hall where a performance of
*Henry V* is just ending. The final chorus is heard within.]

*Thus far, with rough and all-unable pen,*
*  Our bending author hath pursued the story;*
*In little room confining mighty men,*
*  Mangling by starts the full course of their glory.*
*Small time, but in that small most greatly liv'd*
*  This star of England: Fortune made his sword,*
*By which the world's best garden he achiev'd,*
*  And of it left his son imperial lord.*
*Henry the Sixth, in infant bands crown'd King*
*  Of France and England, did this king succeed;*
*Whose state so many had the managing,*
*  That they lost France and made his England bleed:*
*Which oft our stage hath shown; and, for their sake,*
*In your fair minds let this acceptance take.*

[The noise of applause and many voices. Some of the players enter]

FIRST ACTOR: This way, this way.

SECOND ACTOR:                            Will she come down?

FIRST ACTOR:                                         Anon.
She'll come with Will. What, did you see her smile?

THIRD ACTOR: Aye, at ' the youth of England are on fire '.

FIRST ACTOR: And ' gracious empress '.
                              Aye, she nodded then:
As to say ' So he will '. Back, back, she's here.

[ELIZABETH enters, with SHAKESPEARE, SOUTHAMPTON, RALEIGH,
and the Court]

ELIZABETH: ' Upon the Queen! let us, our wives and
    children . . .
O hard condition.' Nay, I spoil the words.

' Twin-born with greatness ' . . . how did it go? Let be.
Will nothing serve you, master, but you must
Hold an attentive scrutiny of our souls,
And hang them out for play-bills?

SHAKESPEARE: Please your Grace—

ELIZABETH: 'Tis the false melody saves your necks, and adds
Its treasonable practice in my heart,
To gain your pardon. Witchery! Witchery!
This is somewhat more or less than manhood. Say,
Have you considered all men's offices
As closely as our queenship?

SHAKESPEARE: Madam, no—
How should not the most eminent height that shines
In the sun's early boldness, and where last
He himself winks to see his coloured beams
Ruined against that snow-heaped chastity,
Take the surprised sight of imagination
Much more than any hill or strewèd plain?

ELIZABETH: Ah, rogue, rogue! Tell me, rogue, what is it
    you do
When you would peer about the presence, find
The ache in the head that the crown's weight brings out,
And the ache in the heart that rivals it?

SHAKESPEARE: No more
Than pace my lodging up and down awhile,
Keeping the active and injurious mind
Styed in his cell, and feeling dumbly out
Into the dark that holds us.

ELIZABETH: Say you so?
Does our best poet guess no more? My lords,
Gentlemen, which of you will answer us?
How is it that these fellows do their work—

Whether by slinking up and down the world,
Watching men's faces, noting down their words,
Eavesdroppers always of the general grief;
Or by mere chance and pale-cheeked inspiration,
Taking the cloudy message of a god?
RALEIGH: Neither, so please you, Madam. Poetry is
A state of knowledge, and a means to find
All men's experiencing faculties
And that which they experience. When some mind
Most perfectly possesses itself therein—
Not for a little hour, as a poor ghost
Palely inhabiting a forgotten world,
In desolation and sad pensiveness,
From midnight until cockcrow—but with power,
Even as your Grace inherits this wide throne,
This citadel and domain of empery,
With a most royal presence, being made
Not so much England's queen as England; when
Some living mind inhabits poetry
In such assurance and familiar rate,
Such plenitude of heirship, all our powers
Come to him, doffing their particular rights
In his immediate universal sway—
All thoughts, all instincts, all philosophies,
All apprehensions, all desires and close
Communications betwixt man and man,
'Twixt mind and blood, 'twixt blood and action. This
Is our first master of it; what he knows
He knows in poetry, and stealing out
Along those channels, passed from word to word,
Translates their several dialects to one
Gracious, serene, and metropolitan style.

ELIZABETH: Well praised, Sir Walter. He knows all things
    then?

RALEIGH: Not with a common and ingenious mind,
  Taking the rich blood's level with a mark
  Of sneaking observation, but his pulse
  Beating accordantly with every rage,
  Shakes his thought free to speak the very words
  That rage is choked with in the man himself.

ELIZABETH: Is it so, Master Shakespeare?

SHAKESPEARE:                    Please your Grace,
  I am no tutor nor no prophet, but
  A common actor of my company,
  Indifferent honest—honest most in this,
  That I have stolen a few hours from sleep
  Rather than let a line go shuffling out
  When it asked mending of my leisure—mine,
  And my will serving. More I will not say,
  For many a line goes patched enough, God wot,
  In the mere hurry of the tailoring.
  Week's wages mean week's work, and I myself
  Have a most marvellous gift of idleness.

ELIZABETH: Have you been half as bold with many thrones
  As with our own and Harry the Fifth's? God's eyes,
  Must you teach kings the way to truss themselves?

SOUTHAMPTON: Nay, Madam, ask him of his latest toy—
  Nile, and no Thames, is where he lingers now.

ELIZABETH: Come, sirrah, let us hear.

SHAKESPEARE:                  Ah, but your Grace
  Is to consider that a player's mind,
  Seeking a perfect subject, finds itself
  Sore let by duty and observance. Who,
  Having at heart to draw a queen adored

By the most valiant warrior in the world,
To outshine Helen—who dare lift his eyes
To the near portrait? but, looking sideways thence,
Finds an old tale of Nile to body forth
What a queen might be; if she lacked the strait
Compulsion—as what queen but one hath not?—
And hallowed frost of bright virginity?
ELIZABETH: God's eyes, and must you be so bold? On,
    rogue,
Let's hear your Egypt. What do you call her name?
SHAKESPEARE: Her name, had other stars beside this world
    Crowned her with ice, had been Elizabeth,
    But it was Cleopatra.
ELIZABETH:            Faith, my lords,
The actor flatters us, I think. On, on.
No more; we spoke.      [SHAKESPEARE goes to the actors]
                Walter, your charge looks high.
RALEIGH: Madam, he does not dwell, as some must do,
    In the continual knowledge of despair.
ELIZABETH [half-absently]: Is it a sin to play with words
    like these,
When the Scots' woman's son must have my throne—
Because I could not choose 'twixt king and king
Lest the land's knell should drown my marriage-peal?
Back, Walter.

                [The actors begin]

CLEOPATRA: *He words me, girls, he words me, that I should not*
  *Be noble to myself: but, hark thee, Charmian.*
                    [Whispers CHARMIAN
IRAS: *Finish, good lady; the bright day is done,*
  *And we are for the dark.*

CLEOPATRA: *Hie thee again:*
*I have spoken already, and it is provided;*
*Go put it to the haste.*
CHARMIAN: *Madam, I will.*

[Enter DOLABELLA]

DOLABELLA: *Where is the queen?*
CHARMIAN. *Behold, sir.* [Exit.
CLEOPATRA: *Dolabella!*
DOLABELLA: *Madam, as thereto sworn by your command,*
*Which my love makes religion to obey,*
*I tell you this: Cæsar through Syria*
*Intends his journey; and within three days*
*You with your children will he send before:*
*Make your best use of this: I have perform'd*
*Your pleasure and my promise.*
CLEOPATRA: *Dolabella,*
*I shall remain your debtor.*
DOLABELLA: *I your servant.*
*Adieu, good queen; I must attend on Cæsar.*
CLEOPATRA: *Farewell, and thanks.* [Exit DOLABELLA
*Now, Iras, what think'st thou?*
*Thou, an Egyptian puppet, shalt be shown*
*In Rome, as well as I: mechanic slaves*
*With greasy aprons, rules, and hammers, shall*
*Uplift us to the view; in their thick breaths,*
*Rank of gross diet, shall we be enclouded,*
*And forced to drink their vapour.*
IRAS: *The gods forbid!*
CLEOPATRA: *Nay, 'tis most certain, Iras: saucy lictors*
*Will catch at us, like strumpets; and scald rhymers*
*Ballad us out o' tune: the quick comedians*

*Extemporally will stage us, and present*
*Our Alexandrian revels; Antony*
*Shall be brought drunken forth, and I shall see*
*Some squeaking Cleopatra boy my greatness*
*I' the posture of a whore.*
IRAS:                 *O the good gods!*
CLEOPATRA: *Nay, that's certain.*
IRAS: *I'll never see't; for, I am sure, my nails*
*Are stronger than mine eyes.*
CLEOPATRA:          *Why, that's the way*
*To fool their preparation, and to conquer*
*Their most absurd intents.*

               [Re-enter CHARMIAN]
               *Now, Charmian!*
*Show me, my women, like a queen: go fetch*
*My best attires: I am again for Cydnus,*
*To meet Mark Antony: sirrah Iras, go.*
*Now, noble Charmian, we'll dispatch indeed;*
*And, when thou hast done this chare, I'll give thee leave*
*To play till doomsday. Bring our crown and all.*
*Wherefore's this noise?*       [Exit IRAS. A noise within

               [Enter a Guardsman]
GUARDSMAN:       *Here is a rural fellow*
*That will not be denied your highness' presence:*
*He brings you figs.*
CLEOPATRA: *Let him come in.*      [Exit Guardsman
               *What poor an instrument*
*May do a noble deed! he brings me liberty.*
*My resolution's placed, and I have nothing*
*Of woman in me: now from head to foot*

*I am marble-constant; now the fleeting moon*
*No planet is of mine.*

[Re-enter Guardsman, with Clown bringing in a basket]

GUARDSMAN.    *This is the man.*

CLEOPATRA: *Avoid, and leave him.*    [Exit Guardsman
*Hast thou the pretty worm of Nilus there,*
*That kills and pains not?*

CLOWN: *Truly, I have him: but I would not be the party*
*that should desire you to touch him, for his biting is im-*
*mortal; those that do die of it do seldom or never recover.*

CLEOPATRA: *Rememberest thou any that have died on't?*

CLOWN: *Very many, men and women too. I heard of one*
*of them no longer than yesterday: a very honest woman,*
*but something given to lie; as a woman should not do, but*
*in the way of honesty: how she died of the biting of it, what*
*pain she felt: truly, she makes a very good report o' the*
*worm; but he that will believe all that they say shall never*
*be saved by half that they do: but this is most fallible, the*
*worm's an odd worm.*

CLEOPATRA: *Get thee hence; farewell.*

CLOWN: *I wish you all joy of the worm.*

CLEOPATRA: *Farewell.*    [Setting down his basket

CLOWN: *You must think this, look you, that the worm will*
*do his kind.*

CLEOPATRA: *Ay, ay; farewell.*

CLOWN: *Look you, the worm is not to be trusted but in the*
*keeping of wise people; for, indeed, there is no goodness in*
*the worm.*

CLEOPATRA: *Take thou no care; it shall be heeded.*

CLOWN: *Very good. Give it nothing, I pray you, for it is*
*not worth the feeding.*

CLEOPATRA: *Will it eat me?*

CLOWN: *You must not think I am so simple but I know the devil himself will not eat a woman: I know that a woman is a dish for the gods, if the devil dress her not. But, truly, these same whoreson devils do the gods great harm in their women; for in every ten that they make, the devils mar five.*

CLEOPATRA: *Well, get thee gone; farewell.*

CLOWN: *Yes, forsooth: I wish you joy o' the worm.*     [Exit

[Re-enter IRAS with a robe, crown, &c.]

CLEOPATRA: *Give me my robe, put on my crown; I have*
*Immortal longings in me: now no more*
*The juice of Egypt's grape shall moist this lip:*
*Yare, yare, good Iras; quick. Methinks I hear*
*Antony call; I see him rouse himself*
*To praise my noble act; I hear him mock*
*The luck of Cæsar, which the gods give men*
*To excuse their after wrath: husband, I come:*
*Now to that name my courage prove my title!*
*I am fire and air; my other elements*
*I give to baser life. So; have you done?*
*Come then, and take the last warmth of my lips.*
*Farewell, kind Charmian; Iras, long farewell.*
          [Kisses them. IRAS falls and dies
*Have I the aspic in my lips? Dost fall?*
*If thou and nature can so gently part,*
*The stroke of death is as a lover's pinch,*
*Which hurts, and is desired. Dost thou lie still?*
*If thus thou vanishest, thou tell'st the world*
*It is not worth leave-taking.*

CHARMIAN: *Dissolve, thick cloud, and rain; that I may say,*
*The gods themselves do weep!*

CLEOPATRA:                    *This proves me base:*
*If she first meet the curled Antony,*
*He'll make demand of her, and spend that kiss*
*Which is my heaven to have. Come, thou mortal wretch,*
                    [To an asp, which she applies to her breast
*With thy sharp teeth this knot intrinsicate*
*Of life at once untie: poor venomous fool,*
*Be angry, and dispatch. O, couldst thou speak,*
*That I might hear thee call great Cæsar ass*
*Unpolicied!*
CHARMIAN:      *O eastern star!*
CLEOPATRA.                          *Peace, peace!*
*Dost thou not see my baby at my breast,*
*That sucks the nurse asleep?*
CHARMIAN:                    *O, break! O, break!*
CLEOPATRA: *As sweet as balm, as soft as air, as gentle,—*
*O Antony!—Nay, I will take thee too:*
                    [Applying another asp to her arm
*What should I say—*                [Dies
CHARMIAN: *In this vile world? So fare thee well.*
*Now boast thee, death, in thy possession lies*
*A lass unparallel'd. Downy windows, close;*
*And golden Phœbus never be beheld*
*Of eyes again so royal! Your crown's awry;*
*I'll mend it, and then play.*


                    [Enter the Guard, rushing in]
FIRST GUARD: *Where is the queen?*
CHARMIAN:                    *Speak softly, wake her not.*
FIRST GUARD: *Cæsar hath sent—*
CHARMIAN:                    *Too slow a messenger.*
                              [Applies an asp

*O, come apace, dispatch! I partly feel thee.*

FIRST GUARD: *Approach, ho! All's not well: Cæsar's
beguiled.*

SECOND GUARD: *There's Dolabella sent from Cæsar: call
him.*

FIRST GUARD: *What work is here! Charmian, is this well
done?*

CHARMIAN: *It is well done, and fitting for a princess
Descended of so many royal kings.
Ah, soldier!*                          [Dies

[After the presentation all look to the Queen to speak. She remains
         silent for a moment and then says deliberately:]

I pardon you, Master Shakespeare.

RALEIGH [to SOUTHAMPTON]          Lost, all lost.
It touched too near.

SOUTHAMPTON [to RALEIGH] Leave Will to make it out.

SHAKESPEARE [kneeling]: Madam and Queen, I have
desired no more.

ELIZABETH: Has not your stage been overthrown ere now
By some rude fierceness you have mocked with shows?

SHAKESPEARE: No poet ever from his fellow asked
More than mere pardon for his insolence
In making their grief audible. I think
Perhaps no poet ever knows so much
Of joy or grief or pain as other men,
Because the sheer wonder of it dazzles him
And drives him back to words.

ELIZABETH:                 God help the wench
Who loves you, Master Shakespeare.

SHAKESPEARE:              Madam, why?

ELIZABETH: Because you poets always slip the end,
The final desolation, the last joy,

In making something of it. God's my life!
You will not slip death so.
SHAKESPEARE:                    Ah Madam, death—!
ELIZABETH: Sir Walter, you who talk of poetry
As if you overwatched her at her birth,
Why is this death that we keep off with lights
So beautiful in words?
RALEIGH:                    It is not, Madam—
Not the mere dying but the perfect close,
The thought of dear completion, and the end
Finishing all the story that hath gone
The round of many voices—boy's and youth's,
Strong man's and old man's—that the tale should stop
And not be mumbled in a chimney-hole
Through many weary winters—this is good,
Told of or heard of, played or sung or seen.
But our own story, our best-lovèd tale,
That we should cease to speak it is too hard.
ELIZABETH [moved]: Let be. So many years the tale runs
    on—
So many parts to act. Is there no speech
To list them, sirrah?
SHAKESPEARE:            If your Grace can bear . . .
Ho, Tom!
    [One of the actors comes forward and, at a whisper from
            SHAKESPEARE, delivers the speech]
                *All the world's a stage,*
*And all the men and women merely players:*
*They have their exits and their entrances;*
*And one man in his time plays many parts,*
*His acts being seven ages. At first the infant,*
*Mewling and puking in the nurse's arms.*

*And then the whining school-boy, with his satchel,*
*And shining morning face, creeping like snail*
*Unwillingly to school. And then the lover,*
*Sighing like furnace, with a woful ballad*
*Made to his mistress' eyebrow. Then a soldier,*
*Full of strange oaths, and bearded like the pard,*
*Jealous in honour, sudden and quick in quarrel,*
*Seeking the bubble reputation*
*Even in the cannon's mouth. And then the justice,*
*In fair round belly with good capon lin'd,*
*With eyes severe, and beard of formal cut,*
*Full of wise saws and modern instances;*
*And so he plays his part. The sixth age shifts*
*Into the lean and slipper'd pantaloon,*
*With spectacles on nose and pouch on side,*
*His youthful hose well sav'd, a world too wide*
*For his shrunk shank; and his big manly voice,*
*Turning again toward childish treble, pipes*
*And whistles in his sound. Last scene of all,*
*That ends this strange eventful history,*
*Is second childishness and mere oblivion,*
*Sans teeth, sans eyes, sans taste, sans everything.*

ELIZABETH: ' Sans everything.' God's eyes, but something gained
    For that ' sans everything '. Harry the Fifth
    Gained somewhat—I hold somewhat.

SHAKESPEARE:                  Ah my liege—

*This royal throne of kings, this sceptred isle,*
*This earth of majesty, this seat of Mars,*
*This other Eden, demi-paradise,*
*This fortress built by Nature for herself*
*Against infection and the hand of war,*

*This happy breed of men, this little world,*
*This precious stone set in the silver sea,*
*Which serves it in the office of a wall,*
*Or as a moat defensive to a house,*
*Against the envy of less happier lands,*
*This blessed plot, this earth, this realm, this England,*
*This nurse, this teeming womb of royal kings,*
*Fear'd by their breed and famous by their birth,*
*Renowned for their deeds as far from home,—*
*For Christian service and true chivalry,—*
*As is the sepulchre in stubborn Jewry*
*Of the world's ransom, blessed Mary's Son:*
*This land of such dear souls, this dear, dear land,*
*Dear for her reputation through the world,*
*England.*

[The Queen rises]

ELIZABETH: Aye, right; you have our favour. Walter, see
This fellow comes to Greenwich somewhat. Sirs,

[To the actors

You have done well and featly—all our thanks,
Larger than our purse lets us show. What else
We can applaud you with, our goodwill waits
To know. Farewell; our thanks again to all.

[The Queen goes out with the Court. The actors follow]

SHAKESPEARE [mopping his forehead]: Ouf!
My God, Dick, I can't stand it; I'm getting old.

BURBAGE: Stand what?

SHAKESPEARE:          Her—it—this—everything. I felt
The links about my ankles a score of times
In the last hour.

BURBAGE:          What do you mean?

SHAKESPEARE:                    Some word

  One never thought of, some line stretched to scan
  With an accent on an awkward phrase and—woof!
BURBAGE: She couldn't have you put in chains for that.
SHAKESPEARE: Umph! no. I dare say not. I never hear
  One of her ' God's eyes ' but I feel the slime
  Sticky about my feet from some damned pit
  In her worst prison. Get these others home.
BURBAGE: And you?
SHAKESPEARE: I'll come when I've seen—someone
  else.
BURBAGE: Come on, Will.
SHAKESPEARE: Yes, I know—' Come on ', ' come on '.
  I'm a free man—free? O no, not free now;
  Never free till my credit can be lodged
  At any stall but hers; that cannot be
  Till she release it. I am damned past hope
  In her black eyeballs and more blackest love.
BURBAGE: If you could force your liking—
SHAKESPEARE:                  Must a man
  Not void his rheum upon his muddy face
  When the sleet whips him? I must snuffle still
  With this enforcèd and despiteful love.
BURBAGE: You do not let this longing stay your verse;
  It is your humour still to entertain
  Its visitation in your holiday hours.
SHAKESPEARE: I would not let a man but you say so;
  For I too can be spleenful, out of heart
  With this absurdity which is the world.
  And credit me it is to mock myself
  That I indulge you so far. I must have
  Some other spirit to clap hands with mine
  And swear that man's a booby.

BURBAGE:                            Very like;
  But, Will—
SHAKESPEARE: 'But, Will'—something too much of Will.
  When did I give you leave to use me thus?
  No, no, your pardon. O it grows on me;
  I am as peevish as a seaman's child
  Crying the night long for his father's arm,
  Who, miles off to the windward of the storm,
  Lackeys the canvas stretched upon the yard.
  Dick, I am tossed at heart.
BURBAGE:                          And yet you write
  Such scenes as this your last in praise of love.
SHAKESPEARE: May not a man veer as a weather-vane
  A hundred times an hour? I have loved,
  Lost, tasted, been bemocked and surfeited,
  Played with it as a rattle, drunk it like sack
  To warm my heart—and gone the round again
  With many another trick and fantasy—
  And all betwixt my lodgings in Cheapside
  And the stage door. Well, Dick, all's one for that.
  Get you home now.
BURBAGE:                  What can you ask of Fate
  More than you have—the favour of the Queen,
  And the mob's favour—
SHAKESPEARE:                  O the mob!
BURBAGE:                                    It pays.
SHAKESPEARE: O yes—and there's its use. No, faith,
      again,
  I wrong it; a's a bluff good-natured rogue,
  A' roars you out with any man, a' likes
  A stamp and a stride and a cockled line of verse
  Making it feel good—and a' comes and pays.

BURBAGE: Well, anyway the street and Court are one
  In praise of you, and you the central beam
  Of our company, the man we look to all
  For instinct what is right to do and where—
  Houses at Stratford, princes' friend in town,
  Walking in State processions, and chief pen
  Of all the pens the Muses ever blessed.
  That's you.

SHAKESPEARE: That's I—and this damned waiting about
  In corners and this thrice damned itch to see
  One no-such-special face—and the usual way
  She moves her shoulders, much like all—that's I.
  Get off, good fellow.

    [BURBAGE goes. MARY FITTON comes to the entrance, and
      beckons SHAKESPEARE with a movement of her head]

  O what a piece of work! O now forget
  To know thyself, my Reason, and be dark
  And quite immured! nor send signals through
  To every bitterness of mirth that sits
  In the topmost gallery and splits his sides
  Watching the spectacle of ridiculous love.
  Beckon no more; I come. If thou could'st change
  It should be to some log, some wooden doll
  Hewed from a cast-off branch; thou could'st not be
  More human nor more fanciful. O too well
  Thou hast 'scaped thyself what thou hast lent of hell.
              [He follows her out]

# PART II

# SCENE I

## SHAKESPEARE'S LODGINGS

[SHAKESPEARE at work on *Troilus and Cressida*. After a while he leaves off writing and correcting and settles down to read]

[Enter PRIAM, HECTOR, TROILUS, PARIS, and HELENUS]

PRIAM: *After so many hours, lives, speeches spent,*
  *Thus once again says Nestor from the Greeks:*
  *' Deliver Helen, and all damage else,*
  *As honour, loss of time, travail, expense,*
  *Wounds, friends, and what else dear that is consum'd*
  *In hot digestion of this cormorant war,*
  *Shall be struck off.' Hector, what say you to 't?*
HECTOR: *Though no man lesser fears the Greeks than I,*
  *As far as toucheth my particular,*
  *Yet, dread Priam,*
  *There is no lady of more softer bowels,*
  *More spongy to suck in the sense of fear,*
  *More ready to cry out ' Who knows what follows?'*
  *Than Hector is. The wound of peace is surety,*
  *Surety secure; but modest doubt is call'd*
  *The beacon of the wise, the tent that searches*
  *To the bottom of the worst. Let Helen go:*
  *Since the first sword was drawn about this question,*
  *Every tithe soul, 'mongst many thousand dismes,*
  *Hath been as dear as Helen; I mean, of ours:*
  *If we have lost so many tenths of ours,*
  *To guard a thing not ours nor worth to us,*
  *Had it our name, the value of one ten,*
  *What merit's in that reason which denies*
  *The yielding of her up?*
TROILUS:                    *Fie, fie! my brother,*
  *Weigh you the worth and honour of a king*

*So great as our dread father in a scale*
*Of common ounces? will you with counters sum*
*The past proportion of his infinite?*
*And buckle in a waist most fathomless*
*With spans and inches so diminutive*
*As fears and reasons? fie, for godly shame! . . .*
HECTOR: *Brother, she is not worth what she doth cost*
*The holding.*
TROILUS:          *What is aught but as 'tis valued?*
HECTOR: *But value dwells not in particular will;*
*It holds his estimate and dignity*
*As well wherein 'tis precious of itself*
*As in the prizer. 'Tis mad idolatry*
*To make the service greater than the god;*
*And the will dotes that is inclinable*
*To what infectiously itself affects,*
*Without some image of the affected merit.*
TROILUS: *I take to-day a wife, and my election*
*Is led on in the conduct of my will;*
*My will enkindled by mine eyes and ears,*
*Two traded pilots 'twixt the dangerous shores*
*Of will and judgment. How may I avoid,*
*Although my will distaste what it elected,*
*The wife I chose? there can be no evasion*
*To blench from this and to stand firm by honour.*
PARIS: *Else might the world convince of levity*
*As well my undertakings as your counsels;*
*But I attest the gods, your full consent*
*Gave wings to my propension and cut off*
*All fears attending on so dire a project:*
*For what, alas! can these my single arms?*
*What propugnation is in one man's valour,*

*To stand the push and enmity of those*
*This quarrel would excite? Yet, I protest,*
*Were I alone to pass the difficulties,*
*And had as ample power as I have will,*
*Paris should ne'er retract what he hath done,*
*Nor faint in the pursuit. . . .*
HECTOR: *Paris and Troilus, you have both said well;*
*And on the cause and question now in hand*
*Have gloz'd, but superficially; not much*
*Unlike young men, whom Aristotle thought*
*Unfit to hear moral philosophy.*
*The reasons you allege do more conduce*
*To the hot passion of distemper'd blood*
*Than to make up a free determination*
*'Twixt right and wrong; for pleasure and revenge*
*Have ears more deaf than adders to the voice*
*Of any true decision. Nature craves*
*All dues be render'd to their owners: now,*
*What nearer debt in all humanity*
*Than wife is to the husband? if this law*
*Of nature be corrupted through affection,*
*And that great minds, of partial indulgence*
*To their benumbed wills, resist the same;*
*There is a law in each well-order'd nation*
*To curb those raging appetites that are*
*Most disobedient and refractory.*
*If Helen then be wife to Sparta's king,*
*As it is known she is, these moral laws*
*Of nature, and of nations, speak aloud*
*To have her back return'd: thus to persist*
*In doing wrong extenuates not wrong,*
*But makes it much more heavy.*

SHAKESPEARE [breaking off suddenly]: Too wide; all, all
    too wide! 'Tis well enough,
This heavy sonorous talk, for what it is,
The solemn argument of mighty states
Disputing still if they be vulnerable
In nature's law or man's—but they might think
The very lines out—no; yet it's not truth
Neither, this way nor t'other—what they could
Nor what they would. What does it need? It needs
The utter roundness, words and what shapes words,
The thing between the words that makes the words
Its colour and completion. Fair enough—
                        [Turning the papers
' Injurious time now with a robber's haste
Crams his rich thievery up '; and there again—
' Love, friendship, charity are subjects all
To envious and calumniating time.'
And yet not—            [He walks up and down
I am come unto my equipoise; my next
Shall trim me level with my past, or push
So far beyond my purpose 'tis too vain
To prophesy what lies there. Passion's dull
If it fail now; it must not.
    [A knock. FRANCIS BEAUMONT and DAVID NICHOLAS come in]
BEAUMONT: Sir, I disturb you.
SHAKESPEARE:               Francis? nay, come in.
Why, sir, and you too; you are welcome.
NICHOLAS:                 Sir,
One Master Stephen Bellot, whom you know,
Causes me to be thus vexatious.
SHAKESPEARE:              Nay,
You are very welcome. Master Nicholas?

NICHOLAS:                               He.

SHAKESPEARE: Be so far kind then as to cheer your
  friend
 With promise made to me, through me to him,
 That, if he marry her, Mary's father gives
 A matter of fifty pounds in dowry.

NICHOLAS:                            Sir,
 Stephen and I will drink your health to-night,
 Even if you shall not spare one kindness more.

SHAKESPEARE: What you will, in my measure.

NICHOLAS:                                 Sir, my wife
 Is set below; if you would stretch so far
 As to repeat this message in her ear?

SHAKESPEARE: A moment, Francis. Sir, I follow you.

[SHAKESPEARE and NICHOLAS go out. BEAUMONT picks up the
         manuscript and sits down to read]

ULYSSES: *You have sworn patience.*

TROILUS:                      *Fear me not, sweet lord;*
 *I will not be myself, nor have cognition*
 *Of what I feel: I am all patience.*


                    [Enter CRESSIDA]

THERSITES: *Now the pledge! now, now, now!*

CRESSIDA: *Here, Diomed, keep this sleeve.*

TROILUS: *O beauty! where is thy faith?*

ULYSSES:                              *My lord,—*

TROILUS: *I will be patient; outwardly I will.*

CRESSIDA: *You look upon that sleeve; behold it well.*
 *He loved me—O false wench!—Give't to me again.*

DIOMEDES: *Whose was't?*

CRESSIDA:              *It is no matter, now I have't again.*

*I will not meet with you to-morrow night.*
*I prithee, Diomed, visit me no more.*
THERSITES: *Now she sharpens: well said, whetstone!*
DIOMEDES: *I shall have it.*
CRESSIDA: *What, this?*
DIOMEDES: *Ay, that.*
CRESSIDA: *O! all you gods. O pretty, pretty pledge!*
  *Thy master now lies thinking in his bed*
  *Of thee and me; and sighs, and takes my glove,*
  *And gives memorial dainty kisses to it,*
  *As I kiss thee. Nay, do not snatch it from me;*
  *He that takes that doth take my heart withal.*
DIOMEDES: *I had your heart before; this follows it.*
TROILUS: *I did swear patience.*
CRESSIDA: *You shall not have it, Diomed; faith, you shall*
  *not;*
  *I'll give you something else.*
DIOMEDES: *I will have this. Whose was it?*
CRESSIDA. *'Tis no matter.*
DIOMEDES: *Come, tell me whose it was.*
CRESSIDA: *'Twas one's that loved me better than you will.*
  *But, now you have it, take it.*
DIOMEDES: *Whose was it?*
CRESSIDA: *By all Diana's waiting-women yond,*
  *And by herself, I will not tell you whose.*
DIOMEDES: *To-morrow will I wear it on my helm,*
  *And grieve his spirit that dares not challenge it.*
TROILUS: *Wert thou the devil, and wor'st it on thy horn,*
  *It should be challeng'd.*
CRESSIDA: *Well, well, 'tis done, 'tis past: and yet it is not:*
  *I will not keep my word.*
DIOMEDES: *Why then, farewell;*

*Thou never shalt mock Diomed again.*

CRESSIDA: *You shall not go: one cannot speak a word,*
*But it straight starts you.*

DIOMEDES:                    *I do not like this fooling.*

THERSITES: *Nor I, by Pluto: but that that likes not me*
*Pleases me best.*

DIOMEDES: *What, shall I come? the hour?*

CRESSIDA:                    *Ay, come:—O Jove!—*
*Do come:—I shall be plagu'd.*

DIOMEDES:                    *Farewell till then.*

CRESSIDA: *Good night: I prithee, come—*    [Exit DIOMEDES
*Troilus, farewell! one eye yet looks on thee,*
*But with my heart the other eye doth see.*
*Ah! poor our sex; this fault in us I find,*
*The error of our eye directs our mind.*
*What error leads must err. O! then conclude*
*Minds sway'd by eyes are full of turpitude.*    [Exit

ULYSSES: *All's done, my lord.*

TROILUS:                    *It is.*

ULYSSES:                    *Why stay we, then?*

TROILUS: *To make a recordation to my soul*
*Of every syllable that here was spoke.*
*But if I tell how these two did co-act,*
*Shall I not lie in publishing a truth?*
*Sith yet there is a credence in my heart,*
*An esperance so obstinately strong,*
*That doth invert the attest of eyes and ears,*
*As if those organs had deceptious functions,*
*Created only to calumniate.*
*Was Cressid here?*

ULYSSES:            *I cannot conjure, Trojan.*

TROILUS: *She was not, sure.*

ULYSSES.                    *Most sure she was.*
TROILUS: *Why, my negation hath no taste of madness.*
ULYSSES: *Nor mine, my lord: Cressid was here but now.*
TROILUS: *Let it not be believ'd for womanhood!*
  *Think we had mothers; do not give advantage*
  *To stubborn critics, apt, without a theme,*
  *For depravation, to square the general sex*
  *By Cressid's rule: rather think this not Cressid.*
ULYSSES: *What hath she done, prince, that can soil our*
    *mothers?*

[SHAKESPEARE returns, BEAUMONT rises to meet him]

SHAKESPEARE: Did you ever meet with Bellot, Francis?
BEAUMONT:                                        Aye.
SHAKESPEARE: A pleasant lad, but something over-wise
  In his first love. I run as go-between
  To find how much in dowry the sire gives,
  A Pandarus of purses.
BEAUMONT:               Send your trade
  Be better fated than your pandar's here,
  Unless my memory of the tale goes wrong.
SHAKESPEARE: I never loved the kind, in love or trade,
  Nor much more there.
BEAUMONT:             This goes?
SHAKESPEARE:                     Aye, somehow; pushed
  Through a hedge or two towards fair-day. I can't guess.
  Years ago since I ventured on it first
  And now again a sennight since or so.
  The first for lack of inclination stopped;
  This halts for lack of—skill, strength, what you choose.
  It doesn't reach that moment when hope ends
  And our despair sends out the final calm

With the true word englobed in't.  O they talk,
But they talk learnedly, they talk too high—
BEAUMONT: Sir, if a poor practitioner of verse
May praise—
SHAKESPEARE: You wrong yourself too much.  No .. no ..
I am stifled with it.  See you, when at first
The sun we call Apollo strikes on us
Forth peep the primroses and gillyflowers,
Up get the cowmen, out run serving-boys,
All the morn's busy.  Then comes change; the voice
That once went singing talks of policies,
Heroes; conceiving morals, values, scope
For goodman Thought to set his household up
And push his business further.  What's beyond?
What's in the sun's self, the vastidity
And circumambulation of that world
Which lights the rest?  I don't misjudge my play.
There's freshness in it, youth and decent age;
But the last secret—but age touched with youth,
Ripeness of being, ripeness of poetry;
No longer life transmuted into words,
But words transmuted into life and veined
From the blood at the centre, having one beat with that;
Immortal not with poor everlastingness
But out of starry knowledge into . . . stuff—
That's not there.  Well, you needed me?
BEAUMONT:                                    Nay, sir,
Only you promised Jack you'd overlook—
SHAKESPEARE: O *The Two Kinsmen*? Why aye, give it me.
BEAUMONT: Not to be troublesome—
SHAKESPEARE:                          What, you and I?
No more than Master Bellot with his pounds,

And yet a little more for friendship's sake.

BEAUMONT: You do not walk yet?

SHAKESPEARE:                    No, I work.  Farewell.

BEAUMONT: Farewell, and our best service.    [He goes

SHAKESPEARE:                              To it once more.
Some argument past the wise Ulysses, some
Signification of the passionate coil
That is Troilus' self, now some most cunning word.


' What hath she done, prince, that can soil our mothers? '
' Nothing, unless '— too low; the swell, the swell . . .


' What hath she done, prince, that can soil our mothers? '
' Nothing at all; it was not she . . .'


' Nothing at all; she was not here nor . . .'


' What hath she done, prince, that can soil our mothers? '


*Nothing at all, unless that this were she.*
                              [He begins to write it down

## SCENE II

## A ROOM AT THE MERMAID

[SHAKESPEARE, JONSON, BURBAGE, at one table. SIR TOBY BELCH and SIR ANDREW AGUECHEEK at another.]

SIR TOBY BELCH: *Marian, I say! a stoup of wine!*

[Enter Clown]

SIR ANDREW AGUECHEEK: *Here comes the fool, i' faith.*

CLOWN: *How now, my hearts! Did you never see the picture of 'we three'?*

SIR TOBY BELCH: *Welcome, ass. Now let's have a catch.*

SIR ANDREW AGUECHEEK: *By my troth, the fool has an excellent breast. I had rather than forty shillings I had such a leg, and so sweet a breath to sing, as the fool has. In sooth, thou wast in very gracious fooling last night, when thou spokest of Pigrogromitus, of the Vapians passing the equinoctial of Queubus: 'twas very good, i' faith. I sent thee sixpence for thy leman: hadst it?*

CLOWN: *I did impeticos thy gratillity; for Malvolio's nose is no whipstock: my lady has a white hand, and the Myrmidons are no bottle-ale houses.*

SIR ANDREW AGUECHEEK: *Excellent! why, this is the best fooling, when all is done. Now, a song.*

SIR TOBY BELCH: *Come on; there is sixpence for you: let's have a song.*

SIR ANDREW AGUECHEEK: *There's a testril of me too: if one knight give a—*

CLOWN: *Would you have a love-song, or a song of good life?*

SIR TOBY BELCH: *A love-song, a love-song.*

SIR ANDREW AGUECHEEK: *Ay, ay; I care not for good life.*

G 2

CLOWN: *O mistress mine! where are you roaming?*
*O! stay and hear; your true love's coming,*
*That can sing both high and low.*
*Trip no further, pretty sweeting;*
*Journeys end in lovers meeting,*
*Every wise man's son doth know.*

SIR ANDREW AGUECHEEK: *Excellent good, i' faith.*

SIR TOBY BELCH: *Good, good.*

CLOWN: *What is love? 'tis not hereafter;*
*Present mirth hath present laughter;*
*What's to come is still unsure:*
*In delay there lies no plenty;*
*Then come kiss me, sweet and twenty,*
*Youth's a stuff will not endure.*

SIR ANDREW AGUECHEEK: *A mellifluous voice, as I am true knight.*

SIR TOBY BELCH: *A contagious breath.*

SIR ANDREW AGUECHEEK: *Very sweet and contagious, i' faith.*

SIR TOBY BELCH: *To hear by the nose, it is dulcet in contagion. But shall we make the welkin dance indeed? Shall we rouse the night-owl in a catch that will draw three souls out of one weaver? Shall we do that?*

SIR ANDREW AGUECHEEK: *An you love me, let's do't: I am dog at a catch.*

CLOWN: *By'r lady, sir, and some dogs will catch well.*

SIR ANDREW AGUECHEEK: *Most certain. Let our catch be, 'Thou knave'.*

CLOWN: *'Hold thy peace, thou knave,' knight? I shall be constrain'd in't to call thee knave, knight.*

SIR ANDREW AGUECHEEK: *'Tis not the first time I have con-*

*strain'd one to call me knave. Begin, fool: it begins, ' Hold thy peace'.*

CLOWN: *I shall never begin if I hold my peace.*

SIR ANDREW AGUECHEEK: *Good, i' faith. Come, begin.*

[They sing a catch

CLOWN: *Beshrew me, the knight's in admirable fooling.*

SIR ANDREW AGUECHEEK: *Ay, he does well enough if he be disposed, and so do I too; he does it with a better grace, but I do it more natural.*                     [They drift out

BURBAGE [looking at SHAKESPEARE and quoting]: *O God! that men should put an enemy in their mouths to steal away their brains; that we should, with joy, pleasance, revel, and applause, transform ourselves into beasts.*

JONSON: That's true too; but a man should take his drink
Most like, as all could do, a man whose mind
Uses his habits to his profit, skims
The cream o' the milk, and lets the jug stand by
For thirsty neighbours.

SHAKESPEARE:              ' Should.' Ben, you were made
For a wise pulpiter.

JONSON:              So were not you.

SHAKESPEARE: I thank God for it.

JONSON:                     Do you so—thank God
That you have never tried to turn a man
From his foul ways, and what he loves too well,
To cleaner? Honest men must needs be clean.

SHAKESPEARE: The only thing I have against you, Ben,
Isn't your doing; you've the rarest touch
Of old moralities in your humours—aye,
I almost see the Vice jump out at last
Scolding the devil to hell.

JONSON:                     That's the Old Faith

That works in me—you've neither the old nor new,
Good Catholic nor good Puritan.
SHAKESPEARE:                    Why no,
I learned my craft upon another bench
From quite another master, than your bluff,
Honest, broad-shouldered master right-and-wrong.
JONSON: Meaning—
SHAKESPEARE:          Even now I cannot think of him
But with a secret melancholy, him,
I mean, who was a greater then than I,
And might be greater now, had he been met
By no two surly ruffians; who still kept
His eager eyes on knowledge, his swift feet
Spurning the paltry pavements for the air
They loved so—Marlowe.
BURBAGE:                         Aye; he died the year
Before we went to Greenwich first.
SHAKESPEARE:                         He was
All excellency, he was my sole friend
When I was young, and my great master. Now
There are moments when my heart beats through my
    veins
Those unkind tidings as if all were new—
Marlowe is dead, and as one dazed by the moon
I stagger at it.
JONSON:          He died in a brawl?
SHAKESPEARE:                         He died—
Let it rest there. . . . He died of that excess
Wherein his mighty heart, beating its way
About the weakness of the thinning air
Beyond the stars, plunged like a falling star
Through the great void that took him.

BURBAGE:                               All's a void
Beyond our natural shutting-up of eyes.
Neither of you two, you the Catholic
Or you the poet, can instruct me there.
JONSON: Go to a priest—if you can find a priest
Hid in a cellar; go to the Spanish lord's
New chaplain.
SHAKESPEARE:     All ends somehow. I would have
No huddled-up and scrabbling end of life,
Leaving all things put off to the last, as some
Schoolboy sits gabbling i' the morning o'er
His book ere yet he gets himself to school
Half-knowing it. Week's work, week's pay, week's end.
                    [Singers heard without]
By your leave, my friends. Maria, bring them in. [They enter
Well met, good fellows. What, can you sing a verse
After a glance at it?
FIRST SINGER:          Master, if it go
Tunefully—is there music?
SHAKESPEARE:                          No, not yet.
   [He gives them a paper. They gather round, examining and
                    whispering]
Well, can you do it? or hath learning now
Stolen the natural instinct from our hearts
To make a song of any likely words?
FIRST SINGER: Why, aye, we'll try it.
SHAKESPEARE:                     On then; you'll do well.
                    [They sing]
   *Fear no more the heat o' the sun,*
      *Nor the furious winter's rages;*
   *Thou thy worldly task hast done,*
      *Home art gone, and ta'en thy wages;*

*Golden lads and girls all must,*
*As chimney-sweepers, come to dust.*

*Fear no more the frown o' the great,*
   *Thou art past the tyrant's stroke:*
*Care no more to clothe and eat;*
   *To thee the reed is as the oak:*
*The sceptre, learning, physic, must*
*All follow this, and come to dust.*

*Fear no more the lightning-flash,*
   *Nor the all-dreaded thunder-stone;*
*Fear not slander, censure rash;*
   *Thou hast finished joy and moan:*
*All lovers young, all lovers must*
*Consign to thee, and come to dust.*

    [SHAKESPEARE gives them money and they go out]

BURBAGE: That's a new song?

SHAKESPEARE:               Aye.

JONSON:                     An old song, I think.
All men have known it.

BURBAGE:               No man has known more.
But there's a speech, Will, in another play,
Your *Measure for Measure*, that I got by heart
Not for the acting but for the mere dread,
A thing I keep to love and shudder at—

             [He rises and speaks it]

   *Ay, but to die, and go we know not where;*
   *To lie in cold obstruction and to rot;*
   *This sensible warm motion to become*
   *A kneaded clod; and the delighted spirit*
   *To bathe in fiery floods, or to reside*
   *In thrilling region of thick-ribbed ice;*

*To be imprison'd in the viewless winds,*
*And blown with restless violence round about*
*The pendant world; or to be worse than worst*
*Of those that lawless and incertain thoughts*
*Imagine howling: 'tis too horrible!*
*The weariest and most loathed worldly life*
*That age, ache, penury and imprisonment*
*Can lay on nature is a paradise*
*To what we fear of death.*

JONSON: A young fool in a dungeon whining out
  That his dear body, which is all he knows,
  Having no hint of the victorious mind,
  And lesser as a Christian man than souls
  Such as great Seneca and wise Plutarch were:
  That this most cherished body, which the stews,
  And well-served victuals, and warm sheets by night,
  Made him enjoy, should go into the dark
  Sobbing for all the good it leaves behind!
  Will, your young heroes are the loathliest crew.

SHAKESPEARE: Take them for what they are—heroes;
    naught else.

JONSON: You take no trouble with your plays.

SHAKESPEARE:                          My God!
  I take no trouble! I—who spend more time
  Coaxing a vicious troublesome little noun
  Into its place between two adjectives
  Than you did over all your comedies—
  At least, to hear them grunt the verse out.

JONSON.                          Grunt!

SHAKESPEARE: Grunt.   O your prose—that's well, but
    poetry—
  Ben, you have hit it once or twice by chance,

You don't know what it is.

JONSON:                          At least, I keep
A decent line with history.

SHAKESPEARE:                     So do I
If I remember and have time enough.
But it's not so that plays are written.

BURBAGE:                         Not yours.

SHAKESPEARE: Well, no—not mine then.

BURBAGE:              How do you write your plays?

SHAKESPEARE: Sometimes because a pretty story cries
In my ear for telling on a gay bright stage;
And sometimes for some notion that has crept
Into my brain by night of how a man
Might be or do this, that, or the other, and show
What happens to the mind when that is done;
And sometimes—to put other people right.

BURBAGE: Will!

JONSON:          Doubtless! Me, now?

SHAKESPEARE:                     O no, Ben, not you.
You know that play that came out t'other day—
*King Leir?*—there's chances gone a-begging; there
The fellow got an old deserted king
Out in the country, in a thunderstorm,
With a murderer after him; where all he did
Was to cry out on hell and brimstone, how
It wasn't right to kill a man—boom, boom,
Goes thunder; wouldn't you like to go to heaven?
Boom, boom; but kill me if you must—boom, boom,
Till honest murderer thinks that thunder's sent
To damn him past redemption and runs off.—
I'll show him how to write.

BURBAGE:                     What will you do?

SHAKESPEARE: It was a window opened; think—he goes,
An outspurned royalty, from his daughter's hearth,
Swelling, high-vexed, and nigh to madness; think—
Not madness only, but all things at once
Dissolving in a general horror; think—
This very being, this manhood, that we are,
Breaking; our beating centres dispossest
And all our voices and concerns of life
Eccentric, underivable, dismayed,
Till they have changed past knowing; to which end—
As which of you has not feared madness once,
However staunch you sit?—I will have one
On either side of kingship's toppling brain:
One—a poor born fool, a mad innocent,
A world without direction; one a world
Of fierceness, nakedness, and dancing rags—
And all three worlds sent spinning in a sky
Wherethrough the greater elements dissolve
Even as the lesser. O and all around
High and incestuous and possessive thoughts
And some few steady fools amid the storm
Blundering to shelter. You have known it then,
How near the pit we are?
BURBAGE:                          Go not too near.
SHAKESPEARE: Then the bare heart should crack; then
    the full main
Of being, in an uncanonical haste,
Crawling with greedy, rash, and mountainous waves,
Pre-empt upon the mind's occasion, thwart
The type of manhood, and there force in him,
Behind the ungovernable tricks of speech,
Such blinding fracture of intelligence

As makes the play. But that's for evening time.
I'm for the theatre now. You're coming, Dick?
BURBAGE: You're early, aren't you?
SHAKESPEARE:                         Yes—you'll come on?
BURBAGE:                                           Yes,
In another quarter of an hour.
SHAKESPEARE:                    Good. Farewell,
My learnèd Ben!
JONSON:           Farewell, my unschooled Will:
              [SHAKESPEARE goes out]
What is it goes there?
BURBAGE:                    That's what I ask myself
When I've been sitting with him.
JONSON:                         Indolent
But alert if need shall call him; full of jest,
But if one gives, as talk runs, a glance back
To find his silence out, there sits a dim
Shadow of melancholy on his face;
No learning, no philosophy, yet a knack
Of bringing all a philosophic school
Into a phrase.
BURBAGE:      It is his poetry
Searches our hearts out. Do you know the play
He goes down to rehearse this afternoon
Ere it's presented at the Inns of Court?
JONSON: *Macbeth?* no.
BURBAGE:                Ben, I think sometimes this man,
Will Shakespeare, is not all so much a man
As the wise earth speaking aloud; so fair,
In such a supernatural wonder, come
His utterances, and with so deep a sound
As if they had beaten down the corridors

Without us and within us, the mid-world
With our mid-hearts mingled in passages
Where only the great music that is he
Goes echoing on for ever.
JONSON:                              But Macbeth?—
Holinshed's story is it? the Scotch thane?
BURBAGE: Aye, that.  The murder of Duncan—not alone
Murder itself treading with ghastly foot
The crimson and revolted house of life;
But afterwards—Macbeth and Macbeth's Queen,
Both in their separate ways cut off and prisoned
Within the changeless horror of a sleep
That dreams of naught but Duncan.  She who held
The imperial queendom of the active world,
As quick, as vigilant, as physical
As the round earth's self, in her slumber goes
About the astonished palace, and heaves up
Her slender hands to all men's terror; he,
Being apt in meditation and in dreams,
Finds all his dreams grow round him till they close
All ways between him and material things,
Immense and incorporeal, and he treads,
His mind sleepwalking, and his heart—no sound,
None, but its solitary beating—through
Clefts of futility and helplessness,
Himself most futile.
JONSON:                          And he laughs at me
For being moral!
BURBAGE:                      But this doom is none
Of our inventions and predicaments
To stay man in from evil.  These last years
He has neighboured with old Nature, and gone in

To the world's bottom; he has been made one
With the metaphysical principle of things;
He is made that primal necessary voice
Proclaiming its vast being. If he turn,
Now, for a fit of craftsmanship, a sting
Thrust in him by some folly of this bad play,
That first necessity against itself,
And bring man's topmost struggle into the hid
Cradle and sepulchre of our common life—
I promise you I fear it.
JONSON:                    He's a great man;
But never was a poet yet who took
The last step into madness—all but that;
That's held from them. Well, Dick, maybe you're
    right.
And yet—for all this largeness—he's a friend
To the common people.
BURBAGE [rising]:        Aye, to a point; but if
Your common people try to cheat him, click!
There's the law shut on them. Ben, do you know
He's never lost a law case yet?
JONSON [rising]:                Well done;
Praise to the poet who can beat the world
At its own game.
[As they pay the reckoning]
                    Well, child, and what do you think
Of Master Shakespeare?
MARIA:                    O sir, I don't think
Of the gentlemen who come here; only this—
He's got the pleasantest voice in London.
JONSON:                                    Aye,
But it never talked Greek to you.

MARIA:                          Mayhap, sir,
  His mouth has said a better thing than Greek.
JONSON: Mayhap. Godden.  [To BURBAGE]:
               It seems this voice that sounds—
  Where did you say?—in the caverns where Etna's
    fuelled
  By giants—hasn't lost its keenness yet
  For wrangling with a lawyer or its sweet
  Persuasiveness for wheedling friends and maids.

## SCENE III

## THE THEATRE

[An early rehearsal of *The Tempest* is in progress. SHAKESPEARE, BURBAGE, HENEAGE, and the actors]

SHAKESPEARE: Well now, the songs, and then the masque again.
Come, first the ' Yellow Sands '.

[A boy sings]

*Come unto these yellow sands,*
  *And then take hands:*
*Curtsied when you have, and kiss'd,—*
  *The wild waves whist,—*
*Foot it featly here and there;*
*And, sweet sprites, the burden bear.*
  *Hark, hark!*
                          [Burden: *Bow, wow*, dispersedly
  *The watch-dogs bark:*
                          [Burden: *Bow, wow*, dispersedly
  *Hark, hark! I hear*
*The strain of strutting Chanticleer*
                          [Cry: *Cock-a-diddle-dow*

Good, good, my Ariel; sing it cheerly, sprite;
And now the other. Last night when you sang
There was a touch of mortal in it. Boy,
Put off from you the growing hint of man
That makes you human; close the opening up
Wherein your future threatens.

BOY:                          Please you, sir,
Is Ariel man or woman?

SHAKESPEARE:              Neither, child.
He is a voice beyond mortality,
Quite other than ourselves; if you should think
At all of that sea-whelmèd father as

A son or daughter should, you go too wrong.
You have no sorrow nor no wonder, nor
Aught but a plenipotential music, loosed
From a most faerie and unnatural mouth.
Come, sing; no mortal! mark, no manhood, no
Grief nor no marvel—only music. Sing.

> [The boy sings]
>
> *Full fathom five thy father lies;*
> *Of his bones are coral made:*
> *Those are pearls that were his eyes:*
> *Nothing of him that doth fade,*
> *But doth suffer a sea-change*
> *Into something rich and strange.*
> *Sea-nymphs hourly ring his knell:*

[Burden: *Ding-dong*

> *Hark! now I hear them,—ding-dong, bell.*

HENEAGE [to SHAKESPEARE, as the song ends]: Will,
   I've been looking at it; there's a slip
Surely.

SHAKESPEARE: A slip?

HENEAGE:                    Well . . . as I read, you made
   Caliban, Trinculo, and the other fellow
Plot against Prospero. Well, does anything chance?

SHAKESPEARE: Plot? [Taking the play.] So I did, by
   heavens! No, Heneage, lad,
Nothing at all has chanced or would have chanced
If you had missed it. So I did. Now where—
Right, right, I have it. Umph.

HENEAGE:                    You could cut it out.

SHAKESPEARE: I'd rather put things in than cut them
   out.
Besides, if I cut it, they don't link at all,

This Caliban group, with the rest. No, they must plot ...
Something must go in ... here, at the end of the masque.
Look, look, we'll cut the last two speeches, so.
Tell Dick to take an earlier scene first, while
I fudge up something new. What now do I want?
HENEAGE: You've got to get the masquers out of the way
And bring in Caliban.
SHAKESPEARE:               Right, I have it; right.
Tell Dick, the love-scene, say, and then for the masque.
                                                    [He goes out
          [The rehearsal of another scene begins]
PROSPERO: *The fringed curtains of thine eye advance,*
*And say what thou seest yond.*
MIRANDA:                         *What is 't? a spirit?*
*Lord, how it looks about! Believe me, sir,*
*It carries a brave form:—but 'tis a spirit.*
PROSPERO: *No, wench; it eats and sleeps, and hath such senses*
*As we have, such; this gallant which thou see'st*
*Was in the wrack; and, but he's something stain'd*
*With grief,—that beauty's canker,—thou might'st call him*
*A goodly person: he hath lost his fellows*
*And strays about to find 'em*
MIRANDA:                         *I might call him*
*A thing divine; for nothing natural*
*I ever saw so noble.*
PROSPERO [aside]: *It goes on, I see,*
*As my soul prompts it.—Spirit, fine spirit! I'll free thee*
*Within two days for this.*
FERDINAND:                    *Most sure, the goddess*
*On whom these airs attend!—Vouchsafe, my prayer*
*May know if you remain upon this island;*
*And that you will some good instruction give*

*How I may bear me here: my prime request,*
*Which I do last pronounce, is,—O you wonder!—*
*If you be maid or no?*

MIRANDA:             *No wonder, sir;*
*But certainly a maid.*

FERDINAND:           *My language! heavens!—*
*I am the best of them that speak this speech,*
*Were I but where 'tis spoken.*

PROSPERO:           *How! the best?*
*What wert thou, if the King of Naples heard thee?*

FERDINAND: *A single thing, as I am now, that wonders*
*To hear thee speak of Naples. He does hear me;*
*And, that he does, I weep: myself am Naples,*
*Who with mine eyes,—ne'er since at ebb,—beheld*
*The king my father wrack'd.*

MIRANDA:           *Alack, for mercy!*

FERDINAND: *Yes, faith, and all his lords; the Duke of Milan*
*And his brave son being twain.*

PROSPERO:         [Aside] *The Duke of Milan,*
*And his more braver daughter could control thee,*
*If now 'twere fit to do 't.—At the first sight* [aside]
*They have changed eyes:—delicate Ariel,*
*I'll set thee free for this!—*[To FERDINAND] *A word, good*
   *sir;*
*I fear you have done yourself some wrong: a word.*

MIRANDA [aside]: *Why speaks my father so ungently? This*
*Is the third man that e'er I saw; the first*
*That e'er I sighed for: pity move my father*
*To be inclin'd my way!*

FERDINAND:       [Aside] *O! if a virgin,*
*And your affection not gone forth, I'll make you*
*The Queen of Naples.*

PROSPERO:            *Soft, sir: one word more—*
[Aside] *They are both in either's powers: but this swift business*
*I must uneasy make, lest too light winning*
*Make the prize light.*—[TO FERDINAND] *One word more:*
    *I charge thee*
*That thou attend me. Thou dost here usurp*
*The name thou ow'st not; and hast put thyself*
*Upon this island as a spy, to win it*
*From me, the lord on't.*

FERDINAND:            *No, as I am a man.*

MIRANDA: *There's nothing ill can dwell in such a temple:*
*If the ill spirit have so fair a house,*
*Good things will strive to dwell with 't.*

PROSPERO:            [TO FERDINAND] *Follow me.—*
[TO MIRANDA] *Speak not you for him; he's a traitor.—*
    [TO FERDINAND] *Come;*
*I'll manacle thy neck and feet together:*
*Sea-water shalt thou drink; thy food shall be*
*The fresh-brook muscles, wither'd roots and husks*
*Wherein the acorn cradled. Follow.*

FERDINAND:                 *No;*
*I will resist such entertainment till*
*Mine enemy has more power.*

                    [He draws, and is charmed from moving

MIRANDA:            *O dear father!*
*Make not too rash a trial of him, for*
*He's gentle, and not fearful.*

PROSPERO:            *What! I say,*
*My foot my tutor?—Put thy sword up, traitor;*
*Who mak'st a show, but dar'st not strike, thy conscience*
*Is so possess'd with guilt: come from thy ward,*

*For I can here disarm thee with this stick*
*And make thy weapon drop.*

MIRANDA:                 *Beseech you, father!*

PROSPERO: *Hence! hang not on my garments.*

MIRANDA:                   *Sir, have pity:*
*I'll be his surety.*

PROSPERO:         *Silence! one word more*
*Shall make me chide thee, if not hate thee. What!*
*An advocate for an impostor? hush!*
*Thou think'st there is no more such shapes as he,*
*Having seen but him and Caliban: foolish wench!*
*To the most of men this is a Caliban*
*And they to him are angels.*

MIRANDA:             *My affections*
*Are then most humble; I have no ambition*
*To see a goodlier man.*

PROSPERO [to FERDINAND]: *Come on; obey:*
*Thy nerves are in their infancy again,*
*And have no vigour in them.*

FERDINAND:           *So they are:*
*My spirits, as in a dream, are all bound up.*
*My father's loss, the weakness which I feel,*
*The wrack of all my friends, or this man's threats,*
*To whom I am subdued, are but light to me,*
*Might I but through my prison once a day*
*Behold this maid: all corners else o' th' earth*
*Let liberty make use of; space enough*
*Have I in such a prison.*

PROSPERO [aside]: *It works.*— [To FERDINAND] *Come*
*on.*—
*Thou hast done well, fine Ariel!*—[To FERDINAND] *Follow*
*me.*—

[To ARIEL] *Hark, what thou else shalt do me.*
MIRANDA:                              *Be of comfort;*
*My father's of a better nature, sir,*
*Than he appears by speech: this is unwonted,*
*Which now came from him.*
PROSPERO:                    *Thou shalt be as free*
*As mountain winds; but then exactly do*
*All points of my command.*
ARIEL:                        *To the syllable.*
PROSPERO [to FERDINAND]: *Come, follow.—Speak not for*
   *him.*                                    [Exeunt
BURBAGE [to HENEAGE]: Tell him we've finished.
                    [As SHAKESPEARE enters]
                         Will you have the masque now?
SHAKESPEARE:                               No—
They're copying out the parts within. Break off
Ten minutes now, and then we'll take the masque
In the new style and go right through to the end.
            [The actors disperse; a few remain]
   Heigh-ho!
HENEAGE:     You're weary?
SHAKESPEARE:                  Not so much weary, lad,
As something stiff with writing. I grow old,
And merely glad that all that I must have
Is the morning walk through Stratford, the slow
   talk,
And heavy meditation which goes on
A hundred summers when I am cut and thrown
To autumn bonfires.
BURBAGE:              I have heard men say
They're growing Puritan down in Stratford now,
Forbidding players: does that please you, Will?

SHAKESPEARE: No—aye; aye—no. Leave to Bartholomew
  Ben
  Indoctrination of mortality
  With the true way of living. Shall a man
  Not lock his house for his humour in it, and bar
  The gates of his garden against trespassers
  Coming to steal his apples?
HENEAGE:                          Steal?
SHAKESPEARE:                                Aye, steal
  His ripened fruit and the garden celery
  And the roses by the kitchen-window—all
  He grew with such slow toil. More growth, more worth
  Than any sly quick-fingered Jack-of-his-heels
  Knows when he nips the pears off. Each to each,
  For still the thief says God a' mercy too,
  Pouching the pears.
HENEAGE:            You mean the Puritans
  By the thief?
SHAKESPEARE: I never talked of meaning yet
  (Beyond what a spate of verse might lead me to)
  More than a prayer for peace and a quiet life
  And some such trifle as you fellows here
  Or the chubby babe that laughed at me to-day
  From Milton the scrivener's house in Gracechurch
    Street.
  The meaning's in the poetry, not in me.
  Heigh-ho! I am more wearied than my wont
  Has been, when need has hallooed in my ear
  For a scene in this sort.
HENEAGE:                Have you often slipped
  A fastening in your work? You drive your brain
  Like the King's post to Dover.

SHAKESPEARE:                    O there comes
To the heedfullest worker moments when he feels
All the fine carving and the careful edge
Of his new cabinet leaning awry,
And a chill about his stomach. Lo you now,
Working upon Othello one fair night,
I woke to know myself in the third act
And the preface, as it were, not over. Lord,
I had to pull myself together and make
The sloping of the rest precipitous
Towards the defeat they slid to.
BURBAGE:                         Nay, it drops
In a single speech—almost a single word,
Which (like the giant in the Italian verse)
Reaches and clasps and takes us through the air
To plot us somewhere in the pit of hell;
Syrups—the midmost word of all the play.
                    [Repeating the lines]
  *Look where he comes! Not poppy nor mandragora*
  *Nor all the drowsy syrups of the world*
  *Shall ever medicine thee to that sweet sleep*
  *Which thou owedst yesterday.*
SHAKESPEARE: A word, a moment, and all's done at
     whiles,
Perfectly known, apt for contrivance. Once—
Folly!—in some old plague, eating my hate,
And stopping, half o'er London Bridge, to feel
What room might be, he dead who pressed me back,
For my poor shoulder, lo all common life
Fell from me, my acquaintance stopped, my reach
(Fantastically governing) lost the world
By an imposition on't; from the whole crew,

  Minutely all myself, I stood resolved;
  The elements abandoned me . . . Macbeth!
HENEAGE: It's well your fellows keep their plays. Suppose
  Iago labouring to twist Hamlet's mind
  And the Ghost preaching to Othello!
SHAKESPEARE:　　　　　　　　　　　　Faith,
  There'd be an opposition worth the talk
  On one side; on the other a two-act play
  With one corpse honourably poignarded—no death
  Drunk to the lees. But all your young men now
  Follow fantastic massacre, and their plays
  Reel with a drunken hiccuping to stab,
  Right, left, at any who offer.
HENEAGE:　　　　　　　　　Nay, your name!
BURBAGE: Your warrant, your ensample! Webster? Ford?
SHAKESPEARE: What, shall I now turn dapper critic?
    Zounds,
  Andronicus would sneeze out from his tomb
  A bloody laughter. Experience touches home;
  Blood's a good servant (as they say of fire),
  A most unnatural master.
          [The actors return with their new parts]
                  No more talk;
  Come now. I am your debtors, fellows all,
  For your good courtesy to forgetfulness.
  The masque now. Iris!

          [A masque. Enter IRIS]

IRIS: *Ceres, most bounteous lady, thy rich leas*
  *Of wheat, rye, barley, vetches, oats, and peas;*
  *Thy turfy mountains, where live nibbling sheep,*
  *And flat meads thatch'd with stover, them to keep;*

*Thy banks with pioned and twilled brims,*
*Which spongy April at thy hest betrims,*
*To make cold nymphs chaste crowns; and thy broom*
*groves,*
*Whose shadow the dismissed bachelor loves,*
*Being lass-lorn; thy pole-clipt vineyard;*
*And thy sea-marge, sterile and rocky-hard,*
*Where thou thyself dost air: the queen o' the sky,*
*Whose watery arch and messenger am I,*
*Bids thee leave these; and with her sovereign grace,*
*Here on this grass-plot, in this very place,*
*To come and sport; her peacocks fly amain:*
*Approach, rich Ceres, her to entertain.*

[Enter CERES]

CERES: *Hail, many-coloured messenger, that ne'er*
*Dost disobey the wife of Jupiter;*
*Who with thy saffron wings upon my flowers*
*Diffusest honey-drops, refreshing showers:*
*And with each end of thy blue bow dost crown*
*My bosky acres, and my unshrubb'd down,*
*Rich scarf to my proud earth; why hath thy queen*
*Summon'd me hither, to this short-grass'd green?*
IRIS: *A contract of true love to celebrate,*
*And some donation freely to estate*
*On the bless'd lovers.*
CERES:           *Tell me, heavenly bow,*
*If Venus or her son, as thou dost know,*
*Do now attend the queen? since they did plot*
*The means that dusky Dis my daughter got,*
*Her and her blind boy's scandal'd company*
*I have forsworn.*

IRIS: *Of her society*
*Be not afraid; I met her deity*
*Cutting the clouds towards Paphos and her son*
*Dove-drawn with her. Here thought they to have done*
*Some wanton charm upon this man and maid,*
*Whose vows are, that no bed-rite shall be paid*
*Till Hymen's torch be lighted; but in vain:*
*Mars's hot minion is return'd again;*
*Her waspish-headed son has broke his arrows,*
*Swears he will shoot no more, but play with sparrows,*
*And be a boy right out.*

CERES: *Highest queen of state,*
*Great Juno comes; I know her by her gait.*

[Enter JUNO]

JUNO: *How does my bounteous sister? Go with me*
*To bless this twain, that they may prosperous be,*
*And honour'd in their issue.*

SONG.

JUNO: *Honour, riches, marriage-blessing,*
*Long continuance, and increasing,*
*Hourly joys be still upon you!*
*Juno sings her blessings on you.*

CERES: *Earth's increase, foison plenty,*
*Barns and garners never empty:*
*Vines, with clust'ring bunches growing;*
*Plants with goodly burden bowing;*
*Spring come to you at the farthest*
*In the very end of harvest!*
*Scarcity and want shall shun you;*
*Ceres' blessing so is on you.*

FERDINAND: *This is a most majestic vision, and*

*Harmonious charmingly: May I be bold*
*To think these spirits?*
PROSPERO:                    *Spirits, which by mine art*
*I have from their confines call'd to enact*
*My present fancies.*
FERDINAND:                    *Let me live here ever:*
*So rare a wonder'd father and a wise,*
*Makes this place Paradise.*
    [JUNO and CERES whisper, and send IRIS on employment]
PROSPERO:                    *Sweet, now, silence!*
*Juno and Ceres whisper seriously,*
*There's something else to do: hush, and be mute,*
*Or else our spell is marr'd.*
IRIS: *You nymphs, call'd Naiades, of the windring brooks,*
*With your sedg'd crowns, and ever-harmless looks,*
*Leave your crisp channels, and on this green land*
*Answer your summons: Juno does command.*
*Come, temperate nymphs, and help to celebrate*
*A contract of true love: be not too late.*

                    [Enter certain nymphs]
*You sun-burn'd sicklemen, of August weary,*
*Come hither from the furrow, and be merry:*
*Make holiday: your rye-straw hats put on,*
*And these fresh nymphs encounter every one*
*In country footing.*

[Enter certain reapers, properly habited: they join with the nymphs
    in a graceful dance; towards the end whereof PROSPERO starts
    suddenly, and speaks [1]; after which, to a strange, hollow, and
    confused noise, they heavily vanish]

PROSPERO [aside]: *I had forgot that foul conspiracy*

        [1] From this point the actors seem to read their parts.

*Of the beast Caliban and his confederates*
*Against my life: the minute of their plot*
*Is almost come.*—[To the Spirits] *Well done! avoid; no more!*
FERDINAND: *This is strange: your father's in some passion*
*That works him strongly.*
MIRANDA:                *Never till this day*
*Saw I him touch'd with anger so distemper'd.*
PROSPERO: *You do look, my son, in a mov'd sort,*
*As if you were dismay'd: be cheerful, sir:*
*Our revels now are ended. These our actors,*
*As I foretold you, were all spirits and*
*Are melted into air, into thin air:*
*And, like the baseless fabric of this vision,*
*The cloud-capp'd towers, the gorgeous palaces,*
*The solemn temples, the great globe itself,*
*Yea, all which it inherit, shall dissolve*
*And, like this insubstantial pageant faded,*
*Leave not a rack behind. We are such stuff*
*As dreams are made on, and our little life*
*Is rounded with a sleep.*—*Sir, I am vex'd:*
*Bear with my weakness; my old brain is troubled.*
*Be not disturb'd with my infirmity.*
*If you be pleas'd, retire into my cell*
*And there repose: a turn or two I'll walk,*
*To still my beating mind.*
FERDINAND, MIRANDA:    *We wish your peace.*    [Exeunt
PROSPERO: *Come with a thought!*—[To them] *I thank thee:*
*Ariel, come!*

[Enter ARIEL]

ARIEL: *Thy thoughts I cleave to. What's thy pleasure?*
PROSPERO:                        *Spirit,*
*We must prepare to meet with Caliban.*

ARIEL: *Ay, my commander; when I presented Ceres,*
*I thought to have told thee of it; but I fear'd*
*Lest I might anger thee.*
PROSPERO: *Say again, where didst thou leave these varlets?*
ARIEL: *I told you, sir, they were red-hot with drinking;*
*So full of valour that they smote the air*
*For breathing in their faces; beat the ground*
*For kissing of their feet; yet always bending*
*Towards their project.  Then I beat my tabor;*
*At which, like unback'd colts, they prick'd their ears,*
*Advanc'd their eyelids, lifted up their noses*
*As they smelt music: so I charm'd their ears*
*That, calf-like, they my lowing follow'd through*
*Tooth'd briers, sharp furzes, pricking goss and thorns,*
*Which enter'd their frail shins: at last I left them*
*I' the filthy-mantled pool beyond your cell,*
*There dancing up to the chins, that the foul lake*
*O'erstunk their feet.*
PROSPERO:              *This was well done, my bird.*
*Thy shape invisible retain thou still:*
*The trumpery in my house, go bring it hither,*
*For stale to catch these thieves.*
ARIEL:                       *I go, I go.*          [Exit
PROSPERO: *A devil, a born devil, on whose nature*
*Nurture can never stick; on whom my pains,*
*Humanely taken, are all lost, quite lost;*
*And as with age his body uglier grows,*
*So his mind cankers. I will plague them all,*
*Even to roaring.*

[Re-enter ARIEL, loaden with glistering apparel, &c.]
*Come, hang them on this line.*

[PROSPERO and ARIEL remain invisible. Enter CALIBAN,
STEPHANO, and TRINCULO, all wet]

CALIBAN: *Pray you, tread softly, that the blind mole may
not*
*Hear a foot fall: we now are near his cell. . . .*

TRINCULO: *O king Stephano! O peer! O worthy Stephano!
look, what a wardrobe here is for thee!*

CALIBAN: *Let it alone, thou fool; it is but trash.*

TRINCULO: *O, ho, monster! we know what belongs to a
frippery.—O king Stephano!*

STEPHANO: *Put off that gown, Trinculo; by this hand, I'll
have that gown.*

TRINCULO: *Thy grace shall have it.*

CALIBAN: *The dropsy drown this fool! what do you mean
To dote thus on such luggage? Let's along,
And do the murder first: if he awake,
From toe to crown he'll fill our skins with pinches;
Make us strange stuff.*

STEPHANO: *Be you quiet, monster.—Mistress line, is not
this my jerkin? Now is the jerkin under the line: now, jerkin,
you are like to lose your hair and prove a bald jerkin.*

TRINCULO: *Do, do: we steal by line and level, an't like your
grace.*

STEPHANO: *I thank thee for that jest; here's a garment for't:
wit shall not go unrewarded while I am king of this country:
' Steal by line and level' is an excellent pass of pate; there's
another garment for't.*

TRINCULO: *Monster, come, put some lime upon your fingers,
and away with the rest.*

CALIBAN: *I will have none on't: we shall lose our time,
And all be turned to barnacles, or to apes
With foreheads villanous low.*

STEPHANO: *Monster, lay-to your fingers: help to bear this away where my hogshead of wine is, or I'll turn you out of my kingdom. Go to; carry this.*

TRINCULO: *And this.*

STEPHANO: *Ay, and this.*

[A noise of hunters heard. Enter divers spirits, in shape of hounds, and hunt them about; PROSPERO and ARIEL setting them on]

PROSPERO: *Hey, Mountain, hey!*

ARIEL: *Silver! there it goes, Silver!*

PROSPERO: *Fury, Fury! there, Tyrant, there! hark, hark!*

[CALIBAN, STEPHANO, and TRINCULO are driven out

*Go, charge my goblins that they grind their joints*
*With dry convulsions; shorten up their sinews*
*With aged cramps, and more pinch-spotted make them*
*Than pard, or cat o'mountain.*

ARIEL:                          *Hark! they roar.*

PROSPERO: *Let them be hunted soundly. At this hour*
*Lie at my mercy all mine enemies:*
*Shortly shall all my labours end, and thou*
*Shalt have the air at freedom; for a little*
*Follow, and do me service.*                    [Exeunt

SHAKESPEARE: All thanks. To-morrow then, and Thursday week
Shall see it ride or wreck. Goodnight to all.
[The actors disperse

HENEAGE: For one who is so gracious in his talk,
Heaving the world off with his shoulder, your Duke
Is marvellous careful of his life; a shade
So active to prim off another shade?

SHAKESPEARE: Why faith, he misses somewhat of the end,
Being something a false poet, something wrapped

In a furred talkativeness: did you not hear
In the first act? They are wrought all of one clay,
These Prosperos and Brutuses—no scope
But the magniloquence of an inward look
That meditates upon their bosom's lore.
They have no outward trick to take the time
But with a most unpunctual nobleness
Slipping the exact moment.

HENEAGE:                        But within?

SHAKESPEARE: God 'ild them, not there neither. Yet, my
   lad,
He reaches either way to something more
Than your quick brains, mayhap, are master of.

HENEAGE: He bears no grudge at least; he pardons all.

SHAKESPEARE: Aye—he falls down there. Yet the play's
   to end:
He must speak somewhat. If Miranda now
Should lay her hand upon Alonzo's mouth—
No, she has naught to pardon. It's too broad
Once uttered, this same pardon. O some shy
Half-stammered invocation of all peace,
Some tender blame of laughter, some rebuke
Lost in an intimate love! Well, God mend all!
                                        [To BURBAGE
Dick, will you come to my lodging? Ere I go,
And that's too soon now if the *Tempest* holds,
There's half a hundred niggling little points
To settle, and a matter of thirty crowns
Gone wandering in last month's accounts.

BURBAGE:                                So much?

SHAKESPEARE: Aye—I've as good a head for figures as
   most,

I

But your man's fist is so damned crooked it gives
Even me a headache conning them.  Ere I go
I'll have all clear—contract, accounts, and all.
I can't come up from Stratford every month
To wrangle if we meant one thing or two,
At least I won't.
BURBAGE:            I thought it was clear enough.
SHAKESPEARE: Not clear enough for me.  Why in my
    time
I've sent a couple of dozen of chapfallen rogues
Bleating  through  London,  sheep  themselves,  who
    thought,
Because I spent an hour upon a song,
I was a sheep for shearing.  Why, ' God's eyes ',
As the great queen would say, she being apt
To tie her pursestrings tighter—a wise queen—
Would they have actors everywhere be spry
To speak the lines set down for them?  Will you walk?
Now, in the matter of these thirty crowns,
I see the opening.  When we spent last May . . .
[They go out, SHAKESPEARE's voice dying away in the distance]

## SCENE IV

## ON THE ROAD TO STRATFORD

[AUTOLYCUS comes in on his way to the sheep-shearing. He begins
to limp as SHAKESPEARE enters]

AUTOLYCUS: Well met, good father.

SHAKESPEARE:                              Well met, godly son.

AUTOLYCUS: Ah woe is me for my ungodliness!

SHAKESPEARE: What now?

AUTOLYCUS:              Ah woe is me! are you by chance
  One of the Lord's confessors?

SHAKESPEARE:                         Umph! I have
  Confessed a lord—and almost a queen too—
  In my working days.

AUTOLYCUS:              Nay then, you must be one
  Of the Old Faith?

SHAKESPEARE:         Of the very oldest faith
  Your grandam breeched you in.

AUTOLYCUS:                         Ah good sweet sir,
  How that rings true! my grandam speaks again
  In my hearing. Now, sir—

SHAKESPEARE:                    Farther, by your leave!

AUTOLYCUS: Well, sir, it chanced thus—

SHAKESPEARE:                              Nay, on the other side
  Is room to spare.

AUTOLYCUS:         This short half-hour ago,
  Leaping out of a hedge down to the lane,
  I missed my footing, sprawled at length, and here
  Limp five miles out of my ending, and a foot
  Twisted beneath me.

SHAKESPEARE:              'Las, poor man!

AUTOLYCUS:                              Kind sir,
  Sweet sir, an arm a little way!

SHAKESPEARE:                     An arm!
  Who would not lend an arm to virtue in pain?
  Nay, a staff too.
[He swings his staff, and as if by accident strikes AUTOLYCUS on
                the legs as the Clown enters]
                    'Las, sir, the staff went wide,
  Twisted beneath me!
AUTOLYCUS:                 Nay, good sir, sweet sir!
CLOWN: Why now, do you beat him?
SHAKESPEARE:                     Beat him? I beat? Sir,
  Since I perceive you are of quality,
  I would not have you entertain so small
  A thought as beating! Mark, the strangest thing!
  He trusting to his foot, I to my staff,
  Are both alike made dullards. See! [He plays his staff again
AUTOLYCUS:                         Sweet sir!
SHAKESPEARE: Such things engage philosophers; you are,
  By your sage look, in the schools, and know what art
  The moon hath to control our spirits, how
  The crack o' the thunder makes milk sour, and if
  The cats that sing on the walls at breeding time
  Sing ever in tune with the stars.
CLOWN:                         I've looked at stars
  Very often; aye, my father is called wise,
  And a' often talks of the thunder.
SHAKESPEARE:                 So it is
  You have a natural air of learning.
CLOWN:                         Why,
  I've made my pothooks—
SHAKESPEARE:         See now!
CLOWN:                     —can guess you a rogue
  As well as the next man.

SHAKESPEARE:                    If there were rogues in sight,
  You'd harry them as well as the fox you drove
  Last week from the hencoops.
CLOWN:                             How did you know?
SHAKESPEARE:                              In truth,
  This whisperer of the sun's dear secrets breathed
  The knowledge of great happenings in my ear
  At a conjuration.
CLOWN:             Beseech your worships both
  To bear me company to the shearing feast
  In yonder meadow; your honour shall have state
  And a many ancient men to sit among,
  So learned as you are.
                    [The feasters are seen]
SHAKESPEARE:      Sheep-shearing, ha?
  That's my true lad of wisdom; that's the pin
  In the axle of the world. I come, I come.
  And you, my limping squire of ankles, you
  Shall join in the flurry with an itching hand
  Kept from all pockets and plackets!
                [He sees FLORIZEL and PERDITA]
                              See you now,
  These young ones are among it! O the fresh
  Dew that no sun can dry; not all the suns
  Beating on the foul sewers of London can
  Bid this not be or eyes not see it so.
  That's the fair prophecy a hundred nights
  Spoiled by the hired embraces of a whore
  Never undo! O yet once more to sound
  This young perfection! O new vision, thou
  Be throned with my best Imogen! little care
  Thou hast for't, but let be.  Sir, I await

The courteous custody of your direction
With all my inclination. Shall we on?
[They join the feasters

SHEPHERD: *Fie, daughter! when my old wife lived, upon*
*This day she was both pantler, butler, cook;*
*Both dame and servant; welcom'd all, serv'd all,*
*Would sing her song and dance her turn; now here,*
*At upper end of the table, now i' the middle;*
*On his shoulder, and his; her face o' fire*
*With labour and the thing she took to quench it,*
*She would to each one sip. You are retir'd,*
*As if you were a feasted one and not*
*The hostess of the meeting: pray you, bid*
*These unknown friends to's welcome; for it is*
*A way to make us better friends, more known.*
*Come, quench your blushes and present yourself*
*That which you are, mistress o' the feast: come on,*
*And bid us welcome to your sheep-shearing,*
*As your good flock shall prosper.*
PERDITA [TO SHAKESPEARE]:        *Sir, welcome:*
*It is my father's will I should take on me*
*The hostess-ship o' the day. . .*
                    *Here's flowers for you;*
*Hot lavender, mints, savory, marjoram;*
*The marigold, that goes to bed wi' the sun,*
*And with him rises weeping: these are flowers*
*Of middle summer, and I think they are given*
*To men of middle age. You're very welcome.*
SHAKESPEARE: *I should leave grazing, were I of your flock,*
*And only live by gazing.*
PERDITA:                *Out, alas!*
*You'd be so lean, that blasts of January*

*Would blow you through and through. Now, my fair'st*
*    friend,*
*I would I had some flowers o' the spring that might*
*Become your time of day; and yours, and yours,*
*That wear upon your virgin branches yet*
*Your maidenheads growing: O Proserpina!*
*For the flowers now that frighted thou let'st fall*
*From Dis's waggon! daffodils,*
*That come before the swallow dares, and take*
*The winds of March with beauty; violets dim,*
*But sweeter than the lids of Juno's eyes*
*Or Cytherea's breath; pale prime-roses,*
*That die unmarried, ere they can behold*
*Bright Phœbus in his strength, a malady*
*Most incident to maids, bold oxlips and*
*The crown imperial; lilies of all kinds,*
*The flower-de-luce being one. O! these I lack*
*To make you garlands of, and my sweet friend,*
*To strew him o'er and o'er!*
FLORIZEL:                    *What! like a corse?*
PERDITA: *No, like a bank for love to lie and play on;*
*Not like a corse; or if,—not to be buried,*
*But quick and in mine arms. Come, take your flowers:*
*Methinks I play as I have seen them do*
*In Whitsun pastorals: sure this robe of mine*
*Does change my disposition.*
FLORIZEL:                    *What you do*
*Still betters what is done. When you speak, sweet,*
*I'd have you do it ever: when you sing,*
*I'd have you buy and sell so; so give alms;*
*Pray so; and, for the ordering your affairs,*
*To sing them too: when you do dance, I wish you*

*A wave o' the sea, that you might ever do*
*Nothing but that; move still, still so,*
*And own no other function: each your doing,*
*So singular in each particular,*
*Crowns what you are doing in the present deed,*
*That all your acts are queens. . . .*
CLOWN:                         *Come on, strike up.*
DORCAS: *Mopsa must be your mistress; marry garlic,*
*To mend her kissing with.*
MOPSA:                         *Now, in good time!*
CLOWN: *Not a word, a word: we stand upon our manners.*
*Come, strike up.*
    [Music. Here a dance of shepherds and shepherdesses]


AUTOLYCUS

*Lawn as white as driven snow;*
*Cyprus black as e'er was crow;*
*Gloves as sweet as damask roses;*
*Masks for faces and for noses;*
*Bugle-bracelet, necklace-amber,*
*Perfume for a lady's chamber;*
*Golden quoifs and stomachers,*
*For my lads to give their dears;*
*Pins and poking-sticks of steel;*
*What maids lack from head to heel:*
*Come, buy of me, come; come buy, come buy;*
*Buy, lads, or else your lasses cry:*
*Come, buy.*

CLOWN: *If I were not in love with Mopsa, thou shouldst*
*take no money of me; but being enthralled as I am, it will*
*also be the bondage of certain ribands and gloves. . . .*

MOPSA: *Come, you promised me a tawdry lace and a pair of sweet gloves.*

CLOWN: *Have I not told thee how I was cozened by the way, and lost all my money?*

AUTOLYCUS: *And indeed, sir, there are cozeners abroad; therefore it behoves men to be wary.*

CLOWN: *Fear not thou, man, thou shalt lose nothing here.*

AUTOLYCUS: *I hope so, sir; for I have about me many parcels of charge.*

CLOWN: *What hast here? ballads?*

MOPSA: *Pray now, buy some: I love a ballad in print, a-life, for then we are sure they are true.*

AUTOLYCUS: *Here's one to a very doleful tune, how a usurer's wife was brought to bed of twenty money-bags at a burden; and how she longed to eat adders' heads and toads carbonadoed.*

MOPSA: *Is it true, think you?*

AUTOLYCUS: *Very true, and but a month old.*

DORCAS: *Bless me from marrying a usurer!*

AUTOLYCUS: *Here's the midwife's name to't, one Mistress Taleporter, and five or six honest wives' that were present. Why should I carry lies abroad?*

MOPSA: *Pray you now, buy it.*

CLOWN: *Come on, lay it by: and let's first see moe ballads; we'll buy the other things anon.*

AUTOLYCUS: *Here's another ballad of a fish that appeared upon the coast on Wednesday the fourscore of April, forty thousand fathom above water, and sung this ballad against the hard hearts of maids: it was thought she was a woman and was turned into a cold fish for she would not exchange flesh with one that loved her. The ballad is very pitiful and as true.*

DORCAS: *Is it true too, think you?*

AUTOLYCUS: *Five justices' hands at it, and witnesses more than my pack will hold.*

CLOWN: *Lay it by too: another.*

AUTOLYCUS: *This is a merry ballad, but a very pretty one.*

MOPSA: *Let's have some merry ones.*

AUTOLYCUS: *Why, this is a passing merry one, and goes to the tune of 'Two maids wooing a man': there's scarce a maid westward but she sings it: 'tis in request, I can tell you.*

MOPSA: *We can both sing it: if thou'lt bear a part thou shalt hear; 'tis in three parts.*

DORCAS: *We had the tune on't a month ago.*

AUTOLYCUS: *I can bear my part; you must know 'tis my occupation: have at it with you.*


AUTOLYCUS: *Get you hence, for I must go,*
*Where it fits not you to know.*

DORCAS:        *Whither?*

MOPSA:        *O! whither?*

DORCAS:        *Whither?*

MOPSA: *It becomes thy oath full well,*
*Thou to me thy secrets tell.*

DORCAS: *Me too: let me go thither.*

MOPSA: *Or thou go'st to the grange or mill.*

DORCAS: *If to either, thou dost ill.*

AUTOLYCUS:        *Neither.*

DORCAS:        *What, neither?*

AUTOLYCUS:        *Neither.*

DORCAS: *Thou hast sworn my love to be.*

MOPSA: *Thou hast sworn it more to me:*
*Then whither go'st? say whither?*

SHAKESPEARE [to PERDITA]: You are the best of nature;
  being man,
I needs must think so, but no more as do
Impetuous and double-dealing youth,
Saving your friend this gentleman. Shall I wrong
So far his right in you as to desire
To be his tributary with my purse
But to some riband?
PERDITA:              O sir, I am stocked
By my own thrift against you both.
SHAKESPEARE:            Nay then,
I swear that thrift is duller than I thought,
Forbidding service.
FLORIZEL:         Sir, she stays my hand
Even though my will outgoes her, and so dams
The full stream of my purpose that my heart
Levels its flood with its green banks, and holds
The horizon in its glass.
PERDITA:         I would have all
My own horizon seen, which cannot be
When the high water sinks, some current sped
Through pipes of giving.
SHAKESPEARE:       Fairest, hold to that,
The largest vision in the deepest flood.
Sir, you are fortunate in your plighting.
FLORIZEL:             O
Beyond all scope of plighting fortunate!
SHAKESPEARE: This single vision is most happy—know,
Young ones, it is a certainty beyond
Anything else of dreams or waking hours,
Whether it be true or false.
PERDITA:        It false!

SHAKESPEARE:                              I will
  Suppose it neither; being what it is,
  It is mere that, and gracious. Grace to both,
  And thanks for this hour's knowledge.
FLORIZEL:                              But it false!
SHAKESPEARE: O sir, forget me. True and false are words,
  And you are troth to things, resorting there
  Into the gayest moment earth has fetched
  Out of her journey. Grace to both; farewell.
PERDITA: Farewell and happiness!
FLORIZEL:                              Farewell and joy!
SHAKESPEARE: Farewell, and always a most quiet fare-
  well!

EPILOGUE

THE GARDEN AT NEW PLACE

[SHAKESPEARE and his son-in-law HALL, BEN JONSON]

SHAKESPEARE: Well; it's been merry to see you.
JONSON:                                    Merry indeed,
  But won't you come to London any more?
SHAKESPEARE: No, no; why should I? Aye, I know your
    voice,
  And bears a score of others here with yours
  From theatres, taverns, lodgings—but no more.
  I am settled.
JONSON:          Will, I think you never loved
  A single one of us with all your heart.
SHAKESPEARE: Perhaps I did not. All my heart? My Ben,
  Where's the gross churl will do himself such wrong
  As to pretend he pitches his whole life,
  All his degrees of nature, all the kin
  That makes him manhood, by the opening door
  Of any kind acquaintance, who, when he stales—
  What's to be done then with the panoply
  Of music and the faithful serenade
  Dancing out there in the twilight?
HALL:                                    Must he stale?
  You underrate the faithfulness of love.
SHAKESPEARE: Not love's, but the kind of love's. Ben,
    I protest,
  Though it sound surly but to hint it you,
  I have nigh as easy and as pleased a heart
  With any casual stranger as with them
  I played my life's advancement with. Who comes
  For a sight of me and a cup of sack, why, well,
  God bless him, and God bless you; but for me—

I would not go—I know not how it is—
A step to draw them hither.
JONSON:                                    I have known
You always were more loved than loving.
SHAKESPEARE:                                         Not so,
  Neither; but where's the sense to press the earth
  Out of her seasonable course, or cry
  Daffodils up over lords-and-ladies, hawks
  Over the farm geese? All's now so much one
  I can sit contented with the very air
  Ruffling my hairs, or with the preacher in church,
  So much a Puritan as he seems to be,
  Or with the neighbour that caps me in the street,
  Or with the white drake scuffling o'er the lane,
  Or . . .
JONSON: —me or any of us.  Give you joy.
SHAKESPEARE: Well, 'tis beyond rather than this side joy:
  And yet, believe me, if I could so choose
  Out of a million and particular joys
  One joy to treasure, I'd more lief have you
  Than any of them all—for memory
  Enhances this love too imperiously
  In the mere use on't.
JONSON:                             You were ever hard,
  As hard as your own Hamlet when he bruised
  Ophelia's heart and broke it.
SHAKESPEARE:                                No, not hard;
  Nor do I now in any wise hate the earth,
  Conception, and the growing of small things,
  As Hamlet did.  Not hard, for I too, Ben,
  Have given my heart from its own spiny charge
  To the full circle of the rounded O.

JONSON: The Globe—or what now?

SHAKESPEARE: Aye, the globe perhaps—
Completion anyhow.

JONSON: Talking of the Globe,
What will you do about your plays?

SHAKESPEARE: My plays?

JONSON: When will you gather them, strike the errors
out,
Print them and give them to the world?

SHAKESPEARE: I print?

JONSON: Leave them, and say: ' There lies my gift '?

SHAKESPEARE: My gift?
What should I do, Ben, giving things to the world,
More than the farmer's man who died last night?

JONSON: The farmer's man—but you are Shakespeare.

SHAKESPEARE: Aye;
Must Shakespeare ruffle it o'er the farmer's man?

JONSON: There are some who think so.

SHAKESPEARE: Let them print the plays.
I will not. What's one fellow more than his mate,
Who each get up at morning, and at night,
After the quick vexation of the mind
Or the body is ended, get themselves to death?
Who chooses 'twixt the twain—turnips or plays?

HALL: Must not a poet be a chosen soul,
A dedicated and elected mind,
To speak the high things of wisdom?

SHAKESPEARE: Aye, I know;
' There are some who think so.'

HALL: And it follows then
It is a part of duteous chastity
To bring his mite to his Taskmaster?

SHAKESPEARE:                          Aye,
God send his Master thank him.  But for me
I have watched my moons out, written divers plays,
Filled with some poetry and much idleness—
*Sounds and sweet airs that give delight and hurt not—*
Now let the poetry and the idleness dung
The earth till earth makes much of them—which is
To make them nothing.  But no brag at heart
Of doing more than any other.  No,
No printing, Ben, as you love me.

JONSON:                               Be it so;
No printing, as you don't love me.

SHAKESPEARE:                          You wrong
My willingness too much in saying so.
Farewell, rare Ben.

JONSON:             Farewell, obdurate Will.

                                        [He goes

HALL: Does he so wrong you?

SHAKESPEARE:                  He will have degrees,
Validity, proportion, one o'er one,
More than the mere convenience of the world
Gravely delights in, as I too have done,
Louting to queens and poets, since I set
My foot by Marlowe's in the London streets;
But to choose wisely, here and there, what toil
Manures the earth to bearing, or contrives
Against the doubtful irony of the world
A thrust beyond its fellows—'faith, son, no.

HALL: This is to undegree the immingled zones
By which discretion rules the world of man.

SHAKESPEARE: O no, for all things in true being pitch
An equal flight; intensity comes in

Out of its crescent labour to repose,
Being for that no less intensity,
But locking up its active powers in one
Charmed knowledge of so many natural growths—
Careless and careful in one act, at once
Lessened and broadened, nothing and yet all.

HALL: You will not print your plays then?

SHAKESPEARE:                          That were now
For a brief interval to draw again
Out of this round, this O, this nothingness,
This all, I gave my heart to—clutch at odds
From the midst of evens. I am no more mine.

HALL: You either are the wisest man alive
Or the most foolish spendthrift under the sun.
Farewell; I must to dinner.

SHAKESPEARE:                    Aye, farewell.
I'll walk in the sun a little and come in.

[HALL goes. As SHAKESPEARE strolls up and down a voice
from without sings]

*When that I was and a little tiny boy,*
   *With hey, ho, the wind and the rain;*
*A foolish thing was but a toy,*
   *For the rain it raineth every day.*

*But when I came to man's estate,*
   *With hey, ho, the wind and the rain;*
*'Gainst knaves and thieves men shut their gates,*
   *For the rain it raineth every day.*

*But when I came, alas! to wive,*
   *With hey, ho, the wind and the rain;*
*By swaggering could I never thrive,*
   *For the rain it raineth every day.*

*But when I came unto my beds,*
*With hey, ho, the wind and the rain;*
*With toss-pots still had drunken heads,*
*For the rain it raineth every day.*

*A great while ago the world began,*
*With hey, ho, the wind and the rain;*
*But that's all one, our play is done,*
*And we'll strive to please you every day.*

PRINTED IN ENGLAND AT THE UNIVERSITY PRESS, OXFORD
BY JOHN JOHNSON, PRINTER TO THE UNIVERSITY

www.ingramcontent.com/pod-product-compliance
Lightning Source LLC
Chambersburg PA
CBHW032102080426

42733CB00006B/389